PRAISE FOR *KEYS TO LOVE AND HAPPINESS:*

"I have known Lorena Godoy for many years as a devoted meditation teacher and inspired metaphysical coach. That her personal evolution has now led her to become a channel for a set of remarkable teachings about the cosmic principles behind happiness and love is no surprise to me. I am so grateful to read Lorena's contribution and inspired by the profound yet simple vision of harmony and wholeness she presents in this book. It is a gift for everyone who opens it!"
—BRENT BECVAR, M.S., psychotherapist, Vedic astrologer, and Director of the Chopra Center Vedic Counseling Program

"I love this book. I was hooked from the very beginning by Lorena's story of how she channeled this knowledge by dropping into a deep state of love and grateful receptivity. The messages from the Masters are immensely soulful. The keys they offer us are simple yet profoundly healing."
—WALEUSKA LAZO, author of *The Gratitude Blueprint* and *The Best Worst Thing That Happened to Me*

KEYS TO LOVE AND HAPPINESS

CONVERSATIONS WITH
THE MASTERS OF TRUTH

LORENA GODOY

LORENA GODOY BOOKS
MIAMI, FLORIDA

Lorena Godoy / Lorena Godoy Books
www.lorenagodoy.com
books@lorenagodoy.com

Copy editing and book production by Stephanie Gunning
Cover concept and key art by Héctor Chacón Hänsen
Cover design by Héctor Chacón Hänsen and Gus Yoo
Interior illustrations by Lorena Godoy, Nicole Godoy, and Gus Yoo
Book Layout © 2020 Book Design Templates

Special discounts are available on quantity purchases by corporations, associations, reading groups, and others. For details, contact the publisher.

Library of Congress Control Number 2020924969

Keys to Love and Happiness / Lorena Godoy —1st edition

ISBN 978-1-7363336-0-0 (paperback)
ISBN 978-1-7363336-1-7 (kindle ebook)

I dedicate these words of love and happiness to the spirit of life and to the hearts of those walking with me on the path into love, into happiness, into the grandeur of the self. I dedicate these lines of wisdom from my heart to the spirit of life that represents the stars, the moons, and the suns that live within me and you. I give these lines to those who are called to immerse themselves in this ocean of knowledge; drink from it as your own truth, as your own voice of expression and reality. My truth may not be your truth, but I give it to you as drops of wisdom to elevate your spirit and contribute to your happiness.

CONTENTS

INTRODUCTION

My conversations with the Masters of Truth began as an internal dialogue with my heart. My loving heart is my genuine being. I have always had a deep, heartfelt desire to give myself in devotion for the good of all and the happiness and evolution of humankind.

Let's go back to how it all started. As a teenager, I began a journey of self-discovery that deepened in my young adulthood as I searched to become a more emotionally healthy person. I was always keen to engage in spiritual inquiry and explore various self-development practices.

After working for a few years and having a short career as a dentist, as well as immersing myself in the life of my family and raising children, I felt an inner calling to get a certification in ontological coaching and to dive deeper into the nature of the self and its relationships.

Unexpectedly, I went through a challenging time with a member of my family. To respond, I was called to apply and integrate all the knowledge and wisdom I had learned. I also stayed devoted and rooted to my faith through deep practices of visualization and prayer. In this difficult period, the extraordinary tool of meditation came into my life—I suppose my soul was asking for it.

Once my experience with meditation progressed and it

was a habitual piece of my daily regimen, I realized that most of the qualities that I formerly found negative in myself and wanted to change had started to dissipate. Meditation became a precious tool for establishing mental clarity, emotional balance, freedom from within, peace, and the awakening of my intuition.

Because of how impactful and lifechanging I found the journey within, taken through meditation, I decided to become a certified meditation teacher. I enrolled in a course at the Chopra Center for Wellbeing in Carlsbad, California, led by Deepak Chopra and his staff. I was looking for a meaningful, purposeful lifestyle. What I most deeply desired was to give and share the benefits of what I had learned and experienced during deep states of consciousness in meditation. I wanted to share how I had transformed myself into a more loving, compassionate, conscious, and evolved person.

Every time I submerged myself in the ocean of stillness and peace within me while meditating, I released physical and emotional stress, past conditioning, and limiting beliefs that no longer served me. Meditation also helped me to cultivate qualities that I wanted to enhance, like purity of heart, freedom, and authenticity. The experience of living connected to my heart enabled me to create a new reality daily. Every morning, while meditating, from a state of restful awareness I would see, feel, and live through thoughts and emotions I associated with what I wanted to be—deep within me. I would affirm: "I am a master of love making a difference in the world. I am a presence of love, of spiritual awakening, and of expansion for those around me and to the world."

In that moment, I didn't know in what way exactly I was going to contribute to the whole. But I asked for the opportunity with clear intention, with passion in my heart, and in a spirit of deep gratitude and trust, as if I was already successfully pursuing my dream.

Over the years, I have become sensitized to the movement of electromagnetic energy in my body and the environment around me. I regularly do sessions with energy healers, skillful people who know how to balance my chakras and overall energy field. In my opinion, balancing your energy is like taking vitamin supplements. You should do it every day.

One day, I went to see my trusted guide and healer, Cathy. During a session in which she aligned my energy, I received instructions from beings of a higher dimension to write every night before going to bed and every morning upon rising. I committed myself to doing this "homework" and started that same night. What ensued over the next fifteen weeks led to the messages that are shared in this book.

This book was written in several locations—wherever I traveled I took my notebook. I started writing in the United States at my home in Miami, Florida. I concluded it on the Island of Margarita in Venezuela, which is my other home in my native country.

Everything that you'll be reading here was written by hand on paper in a series of blank journals and was intuitively received. All were stream of consciousness. None was the byproduct of planning, though I did begin asking questions the further I went with the process.

At first, when I would sit down to write, short statements about life and human existence that were not necessarily related to one another flowed from my pen. These seemed profound but I had no idea where I was headed until I wrote about a set of guidelines for a life of easiness and flow in attunement with our inner essence and the forces of life. The method of simplicity, as the guidelines are now known, is a way of living with no effort, in which every aspect of life is as easy as it is to breathe or blink an eye.

There is no need to force anything. Simply be and do what is inherent and natural to the self, to the body and heart. Simplicity is being attuned and aligned with and within life.

That day's writing session was when I first noticed myself being engaged in dialogue with a higher presence that was sharing higher knowledge with me by way of a mental "download." Left to my own devices, I could not have expressed myself in such an easy way or in such a beautiful form. In an instant of recognition, I realized I was channeling profoundly meaningful knowledge. Sensing that I was being asked to share it, I asked, "Why me?"

The beings I have since come to know as the Masters of the Truth of Love and Happiness (or the Masters of Truth, for short) replied:

Long desired. And that is the secret. Remember, the response to a deep, true desire in your heart that is spread out to the universe, to divine love, will come to you gracefully and unequivocally.

Those who ask for anything in the form of thought—and feel it as vibration of an emotion in their hearts, as if their desire is already manifested—receive; that desired thing will manifest.

Those who ask for something in the form of a prayer will receive it if the prayer is done with faith and trust. Their petitions will be manifested if they're devoted to their own divinity and see themselves as sparks of the light of the Divine.

I understood this to mean that prayers must be felt in the heart to be effective. My spiritual teachers have always taught me that the frequency of a thought combined with an emotion emits energy into the field of subtle energy, thus leading to the manifestation of the reality we're asking for. The Masters of Truth seemed to agree.

The Masters also said:

The greatness of your heart can take this commitment and more, gracious soul, beautiful being, and joyous self.

I felt the Masters of Truth loved me, as they love all of us, and wanted me to feel confident that their decision to communicate to and through me was well-founded.

My devotion to the process of writing morning and night was firm. The dialogues unfolded in a trusted and loving way and were always preceded by me setting an intention that the messages I received would be for the greatest good of all. I viewed this process as a way for me to express my desire to make a difference in the world and to serve humanity as a presence of spiritual awakening.

Over the next fifteen weeks, I received revelations I had never heard before about various laws of existence, qualities of the self, and aspects of life, as well as instructions for a series of daily practices for leading a life of ease, peace, and fulfillment.

All these words and lines containing higher knowledge are a gift to the wise and to those seeking to become enlightened and live authentically in alignment with their true nature. The Masters of Truth made certain I understood their intention in offering them to me. The messages in this book are like a secret formula for happiness, love, fulfillment, and freedom. They are indescribably precious tools.

KEYS TO LOVE AND HAPPINESS

The Masters of Truth are ancient beings who come from realms of love and civilizations distant to ours that have chosen to share the light of their wisdom on happiness and evolution of the self into truth (or truth of existence). The powerful knowledge embodied in this book carries energetic codes for evolution whose origins are star systems and planets: the Pleiades star cluster and the planets Osiris, Usiras, and Galea.

I hope you bathe in this nourishing ocean of wisdom and let its currents take you farther and deeper into an experience of love, happiness, and the greatness of the self. I have thoroughly enjoyed submerging myself in the magnificent and beautiful depths of these same waters. And coming to the surface with an understanding of the boundless vastness and divine reality of the self.

I invite you to embrace the laws of existence and the method of simplicity gifted to us by the Masters of Truth. Let the braveness of your heart be stronger than the fear of your mind as you awaken to the wisdom of your soul and to truthfulness.

Come now and awaken to the truth of your heart, the wisdom of your soul, the rhythm of your body, and the beats of life that pulse through you.

Lorena Godoy
Margarita Island, Venezuela

PART ONE

THE METHOD OF SIMPLICITY <u>AND</u>
THE THIRTEEN LAWS OF EXISTENCE

THE OCEAN

My inspiration, my wisdom waters and master
* of many inquiries,*
May I submerge in the depth of your water,
And swim with the grace of a wise master,
Sharing my knowledge as I get to the shores of
* fertile soils,*
Asking to be planted by the seeds of knowledge
* and love that give life to all.*

ONE

THE METHOD OF SIMPLICITY

"Do you want happiness and simple living? Then let me whisper higher knowledge in your ears. Think of them as drops of love and peace for you to bathe in," the Masters told me the first time I sat down to capture their messages on paper. Because I did not know who they were yet, I thought I was speaking to myself—to my inner wisdom.

Before bed, after my alignment session with the energy healer Cathy, I wrote down a succession of random thoughts:

> *True love starts with acknowledgment of self-love, an unstoppable force that heals. Have you ever asked yourself what you want to heal?*

> *What do you want to give? Is there a gift or inner quality that you want to share?*

Service to others is selfless. It is not wanting or looking for recognition. In serving, the joy you feel comes from connectivity, an entanglement of energy that only seeks expansion, harmony, wholeness, and oneness.

The next morning, I got up and took out my pen and paper again. I wrote:

How could we know what happiness means if we had not experienced sadness? How could we know fulfillment if we had not failed?

Mastering ourselves takes understanding and also embracing our weaknesses and making them serve as steppingstones for our journey into the fullness of our being, talents, and gifts—our greatness.

My goal is to be able to say, "I am a master of love" or "I have become a master of love."

Mastery involves a constant renovation of ourselves on the inside, and that's the beauty of the journey into the greatness of our being. We get to see how far in our full beingness we have come from where we started.

That night after dinner, I brought my journal to the dining room table and sat by myself to write. I started by asking a question I really wanted an answer to. I was still wrestling to find peace with the same issues that had led me to do the session with Cathy.

I wasn't in pain or suffering, I just wanted to give all the love I had within me and serve humanity. I wanted to bring higher knowledge to the collective. So, I asked:

How can I feel for others and be compassionate if I'm not able to process my own pain, my own suffering, and not be able to forgive myself?

An answer came:

THE MASTERS SPEAK:

In the process of self-healing towards self-realization, letting go is indispensable. This is about leaving space for new things. It's also done to reshape and reorder every aspect of the self.

Stop.

Let go.

Breathe.

Heal.

Feel worthy.

Receive.

Give.

Enjoy.

Be grateful.

***

I was eager to try these simple steps. As I was falling asleep, I practiced letting go. My last thought was of how grateful I was for my soft pillow.

***

The Masters had big plans for me the next day. Evidently, they had been easing me into the messages. Now, they hit me with some big instructions.

THE MASTERS SPEAK:

Make someone happy today, give yourself away and enter a river of joy by sharing your gifts.

There is power in mantras. Mantras can take you deep into yourself and unveil your essence. Their soothing effect takes you beyond the noise of the mind to a space of stillness and peace. That's when creativity emerges, and wisdom starts to reveal itself.

This wisdom is sublime food for the heart.

Order, order, order—in the cell, in nature, in the body, in any being—leads to syntropy.

The tendency of nature, systems, and organisms to lose energy and become disorganized over time is always opposed by a search of a level of internal organization of order in them which is called *syntropy*. It is consciousness focusing energy to create and maintain a system.

The tendency of life itself is syntropy.

***

THE MASTERS SPEAK:

There is a method to have a simple existence characterized by self-love, contentment, fulfillment in the heart, and freedom, the method of simplicity. Here is how to do it.

Close your eyes and go to the magical space that is your inner being.

Place your hands over your heart.

Breathe in love and breathe out light—the light of the Source.

Spread your magic through the light you exhale. It's like a celestial dust containing all the forces combined that heal, and it brings back order.

***

I was excited and had so many questions about the messages that had come through that I began a dialogue at that juncture. The questions below in italics are mine. The answers I got are in plain text.

What is "order"?

Trusting in your own nature. No order, no life.

What is "life"?

The movement of all the forces is life. Life is flow. Flow brings evolution and expansion. Expansion is transformation that leads to contentment.

What is "contentment"?

It's the intrinsic state of the self.

Who is divine?

Those who really understand the truth of their existence. Forgive. Love. Give.

Give the joy that comes from understanding the secret that life is simple. You just make it hard when you don't align with the basics of creation, of nature. Life is as simple as it is to breathe. It takes no effort. Life is a natural process.

Happiness also is a natural process for those who understand the secret.

Thank you. I'm getting it! No resistance and no reverse force against anything.

There is no need. Be simple. Everything will fall into place by its own forces through the flow of existence,

Thank you. Thank you for guiding me, for giving me this gift.

***

Before bed, another brief exchange took place. I began it by asking:

What is life if it is not about giving, being true to myself, and listening to and speaking from my heart? It's about how I feel and what I feel, is it not?

THE MASTERS SPEAK:

There is no failure when speaking from the heart since it is the voice of the Divine.

Cultivate a generous heart. Keep enjoying your life. Be joyful and vital. Your temple needs to move energy, nothing is ecstatic. It simply needs to flow.

Let's be present with each other. True presence means being able to see yourself in the other—a communion of two souls that goes *BOOM!* This is what you are here for, to acknowledge each other from your hearts.

TWO

THE THIRTEEN LAWS OF

EXISTENCE

Only a few days into my dialogues I felt eager to wake up and see what new topic the Masters—or my heart—would present to me. This was a day when my heart was going to explode with love, excitement, and gratitude for the opportunity to bring higher knowledge and expansion to others. I took up pen and paper as was now my daily habit.

THE MASTERS SPEAK:

Every morning, empower yourself by believing in yourself. Acknowledge the qualities you embody and give a little thing away. As little as it might be, this will show you that you can make a difference in someone's life.

***

Never lose the opportunity to live, to make others happy, or to enjoy yourself and have fun. See the good in everyone and everything.

***

Praise others sincerely, it opens doors. Everyone likes to feel acknowledged and appreciated.

***

Stay focused and aligned with your goals.

***

How magnificent and vast can life be when we see it through the eyes of the genuine self, through the eyes of the heart. How much love can we receive from that vastness when we open our hearts and free our minds from the ego and from the need to measure everything.

***

Life and light are immeasurable. There is no container for such magnificence—only the mind sets up limitations. Your mind creates limits and measures because it believes there is a need to restrain you from expanding and fully experiencing your true life.

***

Wake up, wake up your being! You are being called to be greater than you think you are.

***

Think with your heart, your true powerhouse. Use your abilities for good and for the good of all. Create harmony. Create a community of love and empathy. Awaken to your true essence and the light of your compassion will shine.

What else can I give? I asked.

Yourself . . . in devotion. Devote yourself to serving those who want to understand the secrets of simplicity and their existence.

Sometimes life hurts. What should we do if life hurts us?

Be ready to awaken with life. In the process of expansion, discomfort precedes fulfillment. You'll be strengthened by being hurt.

Be glorious, feel the joy of victory of overcoming your fears and winning your "battles."

Trust in the genius within you, as it will take you far.

What if I fail or lose my "battles" in life?

You'll understand them as part of your journey. Let's call setbacks *steppingstones* instead of failures.

Are there laws that organize the Universe?

Yes. There are laws of existence. Those who understand and align with these principles of creation live in simplicity. The laws you need to learn are as follows.

- The law of existence (all the other laws follow from this one)
- The law of love
- The law of the now
- The law of no effort
- The law of order and reorder
- The law of acceptance
- The law of giving
- The law of receiving
- The law of recycling
- The law of service
- The law of investing
- The law of expansion

- The law of greatness

The first time the Masters of Truth spoke with me about the laws of existence, I perceived them as a set of thirteen rules to follow without even knowing the meaning behind any of them. But as my downloads of information from the field of consciousness continued, I was able to see them, due to the simple way they were presented, as principles to achieve happiness.

I also had the chance to reflect on each of the laws and found ways to relate it to me and my experience of life.

One of the revelations that seemed most impressive was the law of investing, as I was used to hear about investing in relation to the stock market but never in relation to self-mastery. And it made so much sense to me when it was offered! I expect you'll feel something similar when you read about the various laws.

The journey within to explore the method of simplicity and the laws of existence is as revealing and meaningful as it is soul-expanding. It guides us to acknowledge who we are, our duality, and the qualities we embody, and how we relate to life as beings. Both through meditation and through working with the channeled messages from the Masters of Truth, I have become a more conscious being, someone who wants to stay connected to, and live from my heart. I have integrated the truth that this is the source of my power to create the realities I want to inhabit. Creative power resides in the heart.

Another law that left me astonished was the law of the now. Presence was a concept I already had knowledge of, and it was something I had long strived to attain in my daily life. What impacted me the most about the way the Masters of Truth presented the law of the now was how easy they made it sound.

The present is the gateway through which we may access our genuine selves. When we're present, we may experience reality from an unbounded perspective. The present is the inner space wherein infinite possibilities emerge and suffering is diminished. I invite you to try the technique for attaining the now that is offered in chapter 5 as an aid to staying present.

With revelation of the final law of existence—the law of greatness (see chapter 15)—it was clear to me that greatness is the ultimate outcome of the process of expansion in our lives. As we grow into our more conscious selves, we embrace our human duality and the qualities that are the best for our well-being and that of others. We take progressive steps in the form of positive decisions and nourishing actions that make us feel fulfilled by our vision of realization. By living from our hearts in alignment with the principles of creation, and with the understanding that we are part of the whole, we naturally become able to experience our greatest, most evolved beings.

An Invitation

As you work with the material you read in this book, I would encourage you to be a witness to your own process of evolution. I encourage you to make time regularly for self-inquiry through various practices of introspection like silence, contemplation, meditation, and prayer, and to allow the true qualities of your spirit, like intuition, to awaken and flourish. Eventually, this will help you live with greater ease, truth, and purpose. At the very least, you'll know that you're a part of the whole and have a sense of ownership of your experience.

There is a direct relationship between the thirteen laws of existence and the principles and dynamics of nature. They also have a connection to human existence. In my own process of realization and search for happiness, I have learned to breathe, to let go, to rebalance myself, to love, to care for nature, to give and receive, to embrace what is different than my truth, and above all, to live from my heart with love and freedom instead of limitation and fear. Now, with the Masters' guidance, I can comprehend the purpose of these laws in helping us attain a balanced, happy life of ease and wholeness. A life underlaid with simplicity and flow.

THREE

THE LAW OF EXISTENCE

What do you want to share with me today, Masters?

THE MASTERS SPEAK:

Endless love, and the secret law of existence.

Unify people by teaching this law. The secret that brings happiness and evolution to humankind. Teach them to love and breathe, to care and live, to enjoy, to live, and above all to exist. Exist from the heart, from magic and love.

What is the law of existence?

Simply be and experience yourself from each individual cell to the joy in the heart, and from there to the soul. Being is freedom, it's love in action. It's all the laws brought

KEYS TO LOVE AND HAPPINESS

together for a higher purpose. Existence extends from here to the cosmos and from the cosmos into eternity.

Appreciation is the key to beingness, and gratitude is its voice. Let your grateful voice resonate with the rest of the self and with eternity. It will reign and it will pervade.

Let's understand simplicity as a way of being, as a mode from which to relate to each other. Breathe. That's how simple and effortless it is to resonate with everything you do.

Take this message to the world and the world will grow in love and rejoice.

When do I start to take it to the world?

Existence is continuous. It is a force. It will take place. It will last.

Every day with every breath, you exist.

FOUR

THE LAW OF LOVE

Here I am. What is on your minds today?

THE MASTERS SPEAK:

Love. Love to give, love to receive. Feel the force of the universe combined with your intention and desire to make a difference. You are our love. You are the chosen for the good—the good of all and for all.

How was I chosen?

By love.
Open your eyes to the sky. What do you see?

I see shapes in the clouds. I see movement, life in motion. What should I take from it?

Ease and flow. Everything is temporary. The process of existing starts and ends naturally. Use no effort, simply be. Be life, be force, be love.

Go out and look others in the eye. Face the truth and it will reign. It will teach you more about yourself and your own truth and love. See your weaknesses as a gift that will help you grow and love yourself.

This is the beginning of your beautiful mission. There is greatness for all. Teach love—no matter to whom, no matter when. Be love. Feel it and follow your impulses.

What you say and what you do from your heart is right; it's simply love in motion. Do it, do it.

Don't judge yourself for being love and following the impulses of your heart. Teaching about the laws of existence is a gift to others, a gift from us and you. You are the fountain and the source too. We are one and one for all.

Thank you for showing me the way, for revealing my path and mission so clearly and lovingly.

Love is the light of the soul and the music of the heart. Express it with truth, live it with joy, and smiles through the world will be. Feel it and give it. It is the biggest force of all and for all. Spread it out as drops of laughter and joy.

Play in your heart and win in your soul.

Take it to your mind and make it your way of thought.

The truth is in your heart, not in your brain. Only those who grow in love know this truth.

It's simple: Close your eyes and take a breath. Feel the magic of life within your heart and spread it out for the world to enjoy and rejoice. Exhale it to the world as love, as the dust of the Divine.

What more for this morning?

Joy of life.

What is it?

Bathe yourself in your own love and you will still have enough in your heart to share, give, and enjoy with others. Love is a cycle of energy, an entanglement of lives and joy.

What do I give today?

Open your eyes and you'll see it. Open your heart and you'll feel it. Open your pores and you'll inhale it.

So, be present?

Yes, into eternity and now. Commune with all. No race, no color, no status, no gender, no knowledge. A family of love and for love. That's what true living is about, embracing all as one. A family of souls in evolution for love and oneness.

Educate yourself. We are giving you wisdom to share and live by but with humbleness. We are your equals in soul, sparks of the light of the Divine. Some grow it, others diminish it, but the spark comes from the same source. This is true for everyone.

Go meditate and open yourself to love.

FIVE

THE LAW OF THE NOW

THE MASTERS SPEAK:

Close your eyes and breathe. While you focus on your forehead, above your eyes, let a fountain of peace dissolve over you, entering every cell, every aspect of you. Breathe in, breathe out. Be there, be aware.

Now is the only moment of existence. It is peace.

In the now, there is no suffering, no alter ego, no other state than joy and peace.

Live each now and surrender to each now with trust. Every now brings boundless extraordinary opportunities for you to create. To experience different realities.

How does the now work?

By means of thought.

And how do I limit my thoughts to the now?

By tracing parallel lines with your eyes. The left is the past, the right is the future. Place your vision between them and focus only on the goal of awareness. That's the now. Through intentional focus on it you will attain the now.

The now projects into eternity and eternity will always reign. It's all and everything. It's void and space. It's nothing and all. It's love.

This is one of the methods you can use to stay in the present moment during meditation, silence, or a practice of conscious breathing.

Is there anything else we need to know, loving Masters?

Smile above all and for all. With ease and flow, silently breathe. Let others be. Your journey is yours, their journey is theirs.

How can I see you now?

When there is less interference between our energies. At night—when fewer people are running their technology.

How will I know it's you?

By the peace in your soul, by the love in your heart, by the comfort in your skin.

Wow, that's bliss.

And by a feeling of unlimited love for all.

Thank you, thank you. I'll know you because of love! I'm in awe! Knowing is easy when guided by you, Masters of Truth. How brilliant you are. I trust you'll guide me all the way.

Yes, breathe and trust. We've taken care of every detail. The greatness of your heart can take this commitment and more, gracious soul.

Today be contagious in love and joy, listen with care and you will see magic. Shine and love, breathe and love.

SIX

THE LAW OF NO EFFORT

THE MASTERS SPEAK:

Make the law of no effort part of your daily life and trust in everyone and in every aspect in every moment of your day and of your life. It's trusting that makes the difference in the process of life, the process of existing.

Life is simple. Take it as it is presented to you and be amazed and surprised by its complexity, grandeur, and order. This order makes life and all its potentials accessible to you when you understand your origin and you align with the forces and flow of creation.

Follow the rhythm of life by connecting with your heart. Feel from there, create from there, and live from there, regardless of the constant movement of things around you.

Stay connected to your presence and embrace your reality through awareness.

Do not control, instead *flow.*

Do not resist, instead *allow.*

Do not judge, instead *embrace.*

SEVEN

THE LAW OF ORDER AND REORDER

THE MASTERS SPEAK:

The law of order and reorder is that everything in existence changes, transforms, evolves. It comes and goes for the purpose of balance. A puzzle of interactions helps us to gain what we have lost and live in the grace of the order and the Divine.

From the atom to the cosmos and beyond, this is so.

How may we practice and apply this law?

Breathe and invoke light in the form of order at the cellular level. Imagine and feel the order taking place. As a scanner, bring your energy up and down your body. Visualize the light touching your cells with the intention, *Up and down, down and up again.* It is a scanner of energy carrying divine order. It's the heart and spirit of God, of the Universe, and of all.

By doing so, you will gain order, balance and health, ease and joy, comfort and love.

Love starts with the self. With the one and only self of yours that is touchable by the light and the love of the Divine.

By scanning your body with light, you'll be protected from disorder and disease. A scan is a chance to rebalance and acknowledge the privilege of having a body.

Also, be grateful. Today, stop and breathe a few times during your day. Look around and see the Divine in others. You'll feel it. Don't judge. Just love and exist in harmony. You'll be where the light and expansion is.

Gather together, share this practice, meditate in unison, and be present with each other. Listen carefully, with your hearts open to one another, without judgment. Be supportive, but let people do things for themselves, so they can learn. We are all wise and evolving into our greatness. There is a timing and a moment for each and all.

Breathe and give time to everyone and everything. Love each other. You are a family of beautiful souls, together for the purpose of happiness. Understanding your purpose is part of your evolution and learning in this journey.

Go, be you. Be love. Be joy.

EIGHT

THE LAW OF ACCEPTANCE

THE MASTERS SPEAK:

The law of acceptance is being who you really are and experiencing everything as it really is. Not trying to change or resist any aspect of any event and of your own being, that's the moment of acceptance.

As you accept things and people as they are, you let go of the need of the mind to control. And there is where you cross the fine line of the genuine truth of yourself. Which is also the truth of the other. This exact moment is when you really accept. It's when you are able to see yourself in others, as they are, with their good and bad. As one with each other. As oneness.

Acceptance is about understanding the essence of life, the mystery of existence, the beauty of the self, and the greatness of the heart.

The moment you get in touch with your heart, you are able to accept and also to be in communion with the other, as one.

Intentionally see the good in the other that you seek and want for yourself. Create for the other the happiness, good, and treasures of the heart that you want for yourself.

NINE

THE LAW OF GIVING

THE MASTERS SPEAK:

The law of giving requires detachment from the ego of your human self. It frees you from the need to control your gifts instead of enjoying them with your heart and giving them away to others. The act of giving love carries the force of inspiration and movement towards a feeling of inner satisfaction. Giving is effortless when done from the heart.

Align with your essence, discover your gifts, and share them with grace and generosity for common fulfillment. The law of giving is related to the principle of the infinite. To the boundless desire to share, to fulfill, and to create.

To create what?

Joy in the heart, satisfaction in the self, glory in the soul, and contentment in the whole.

How does this law work?

You open your heart and acknowledge a talent or gift you possess and share it for the good of others, not necessarily in need. The act of giving is more powerful and meaningful when you are giving to a person because you are able to see the potential within them instead of the lack or scarcity.

If you are giving a material gift, offer it with purpose and with your heart, honoring the good and the potential of enjoyment and fulfillment in the other instead of feeling it within yourself. The law is about how blissful and happy you are, as well as experiencing the joy and gratitude of the receiver of your gifts.

Giving yourself in true presence to others creates synergy and communion with them. Here, the ultimate goals, as with the goals of the other laws, are oneness, peace, and bliss.

How may we give these things?

Through love and compassion.

TEN

THE LAW OF RECEIVING

THE MASTERS SPEAK:

The law of receiving is opening your heart to the grace of God and the Divine, and feeling worthy, and also multiplying your blessings for others.

For example: if you receive a blessing, give double. If you get two, give four. Receiving is the principle of doubling everything. Receiving is the mirror image of giving, and many images projecting and existing at the same time in different planes and dimensions.

Open your heart and you will receive. Through freeing your mind of limitation, you will be able to appreciate what you receive.

Unveil your soul and you will feel worthy of receiving the gifts of life. The law of receiving is in alignment with the principles of the movement of things in nature.

Receiving starts with the sense of self-worthiness. Empty yourself of the emotions and limiting beliefs that aren't helping you to live a life of true connection or of love and freedom from within. So that you can open yourself to the new, to the fresh, clear yourself of negativity and host the positive qualities of the self: self-love, worthiness, peace, joy, gratitude, and courage of the heart. As you accept your own worth, blessings will come to you.

In receiving, worthiness is the gateway or portal, abundance the sustainable force, and gratitude the key.

ELEVEN

THE LAW OF RECYCLING

THE MASTERS SPEAK:

The abundance in creation, in existence, is infinite. However, the human mind perceives limitations in its domain. Therefore, there is a need to multiply what existence has generously offered you.

How do we multiply it?

Through recycling. In this manner, you generate more abundance and opportunities, and give more life to that which already is alive.

Existence was created for you to enjoy. The oceans, lands, and species of animals will be safe and nourished by your consciousness and care. Recycling is a means to express love and gratitude to the natural world that has nourished you.

TWELVE

THE LAW OF SERVICE

THE MASTERS SPEAK:

Service is a calling of the heart. In selfless service resides the joy of a generous heart and an altruistic person. Serving others requires loving yourself first and acknowledging your essence and qualities of your heart, as these aspects that define you as a whole being (mind, body, and soul). As you connect to your heart, your desire to share what gives you joy in living and a sense of worthiness will be expressed by default as a calling of your soul. The rewards of serving others without expectations or recognition are experienced by those who understand the power of their heart.

Serving is having an open, true heart and an embracing mind—where all is one and one is the representation of all. Everyone you give to is equal. No color, no gender, no status, no roles, no definitions of the mind exist. It's the generosity and wisdom of the soul giving openly and freely to generate a greater force and unity. It is selfless giving that includes all of us and works for the good of all.

THIRTEEN

THE LAW OF INVESTING

THE MASTERS SPEAK:

The law of investing is that as you invest in yourself the answers you seek will come. Knowledge will come and growth will take place.

This law encourages you to know and explore the depth of yourself so you may recognize its aspects and embrace its weaknesses and strengths.

Your self is sustained by the principle of stillness, as it occurs in nature. If you experience the silence within yourself, without the noise of the mind or your body being stimulated by elements in the material world, then you'll know yourself and experience oneness.

Investing in yourself means regularly giving yourself moments of communion with your true essence. This time should be devoted to self- knowledge and the integration of existence itself.

Submerge yourself in the gifts of the heart and in the wisdom of the soul and know that the truth lies within you in your divine, true self.

FOURTEEN

THE LAW OF EXPANSION

Divine Masters, I'm at your will and command, ready for more guidance on the secret laws of existence. What do you want to show or give me now?

THE MASTERS SPEAK:

Much love.

Thanks! What knowledge do you want to reveal now?

The law of expansion is the movement of the energy or frequencies of the self toward the fulfillment of its greatness.

You come into evolution with an inner force for growth. Consciousness itself has only two purposes. First, to recreate itself again and again in the everlasting and existing now.

Second, to experience itself as the creator of all and for all potentialities to exist.

So, expansion is consciousness in motion?

In every now, in the eternity of existence.

So, the law of expansion is the permanent growth of the self in every now of this existence into eternity or consciousness?

Through the law of expansion, you get to experience the eternity of consciousness in every now.

So, consciousness is directly related to the law of expansion of the self?

Yes. The experience of the self in every now is what causes its evolution. Each experience is witnessed in consciousness, which is where all exists in the eternal now of life. The self is only capable of sensing its full potentiality in the realm of existence through expansion. It has all the possibilities of existence to achieve the greatest self in consciousness. It is the maximum evolution of the self.

Order and balance bring expansion. Order your systems and balance your mind and body so that you can expand into your full potential. Your full potential is love of self and others, compassion, harmony, wholeness, unity, greatness, and openness. The law of expansion brings greatness and good to the whole.

Wow, that's very interesting, Masters. How vast and magnificent creation is!

Yes, as is the self when it reaches its full potential and greatness!
Expand yourself in your heart and mind with evolutionary knowledge and expand the capacity of your body using the gifts of nature and science.

Thanks.

Rest dear.

FIFTEEN

THE LAW OF GREATNESS

THE MASTERS SPEAK:

Make meditation part of your daily life, of your journey of expansion, of your process of existence.

As you evolve into a more conscious self, continue embracing your human qualities. Live from your heart and in alignment with the principles of creation. If you understand that you are part of the whole, then you naturally will experience your greatest, most evolved being. Greatness will be the end-product of your process of expansion.

Be in awe and you will play with us. You'll obtain the gifts and the joy. As you experience your greatness, enlighten-ment can be attained.

What is the law of greatness?

The law of greatness is that your heart attains fulfillment when the vision of your true self is guided both by your divine nature and by the brilliance of your mind. Any human endeavor resulting in the expansion of the self leads to contentment and self-realization.

The secret elixir of growth is being humble, free of the ego. Greatness also doesn't require effort; it happens organically in those who search for love and peace, wisdom and oneness.

PART TWO

THE BOOK OF REVELATIONS

IN PART TWO, you'll find ninety-three short messages for a life of ease, happiness, and fulfillment. There are a few ways you can read and work with this material. First, you can go through these messages in order, as presented, and become more familiar with the laws. In this way, you'll give yourself a chance to integrate the energy. Some days, you might just want to flip the book open to a random (or divinely chosen) page and see what message it holds for you in that moment.

The Masters of the Truth of Love and Happiness are divine beings whose intent is our upliftment as individuals, which begins with self-realization and experiential tastes of oneness and freedom, and the development of a more conscious collective humanity.

SIXTEEN

HAPPINESS

Dear Masters of Love and Happiness, what message am I privileged to receive today?

THE MASTERS SPEAK:

We would speak of happiness.

Happiness is a force of collective contentment and joy, a shared feeling of gratitude and love felt in the heart of individuals, families, and whole communities. It is a major force of light and fulfillment from the heart of those who understand the simplicity of existence—and for those who comprehend how effortless life can be when it is lived from the heart with a lightness of being and no resistance.

Let nature be your greatest teacher. By following the principles of nature, you can easily attain happiness, balance, flow, and oneness. These principles will help you to adapt and flow with the changes that life presents you.

For example, nature recycles its materials to rebalance itself as well as to achieve order and cleanliness. Trees are grounded and flexible. The soil that nourishes their roots is like a mother breastfeeding her children. Winds carry knowledge, wisdom, and opportunities that create resilience in those who are caressed by them. As you allow yourself to enjoy stillness in the presence of the sound of the wind, you will be able to hear to the voice of your higher self speaking to you through the intuition of your heart, flashes of creativity, and in the answers you receive to your inquiries. Perfect principles rule the cycles and processes of life on your planet.

Be happy, by all means. Your heart wants it deeply and your mind will gain peace with it. Search for happiness every day. Give it in every breath and feel it in every blink of your eyes.

SEVENTEEN

SILENCE

THE MASTERS SPEAK:

Silence is the house of the wise, the weapon of the humble, and the instrument of the master. Those who experience it daily in contemplation, meditation, and stillness experience more love, peace, and freedom than others.

Quiet your senses for an instant and experience freedom from the noise of the mind, from the noise of the outer world. Free yourself of the noise of the collective.

Be you and only you. Free yourself of the desire or "need" to be defined by the collective. Free yourself of the expectations of others, such as your parents, spouse, or your children. Be your greatest, most loving, happiest, and wisest self.

Measure your happiness by the degree of contentment you feel. You know this feeling of being at ease, of being in the right place at the right moment to serve a beneficial purpose.

Silence will help you experience the love within so that you may show and spread it outwardly as sparks of light.

EIGHTEEN

FLEXIBILITY

THE MASTERS SPEAK:

We wish to speak to you of flexibility of thought and your point of view about life.

Accept every word, every opinion, every thought, and every being as a different force—a new expression of life. Your world is a diverse world. It has room to accommodate all and all of all. Be magnificent in your heart and embrace a diversity of thoughts, colors, ideas, experiences, and processes. It is time for people to coexist in a world of understanding, tolerance, and love, a world of respect and inclusiveness, so you can share the gifts of the planet that is your home and live in comfort and peace with each other.

Your world is becoming the realm of the evolved, the realm of the Masters of Love and of the free ones.

NINETEEN

LOVE ABOVE ALL ELSE

THE MASTERS SPEAK:

What is on your mind today? What is in your heart?

Glorious feelings of gratitude for all, for creation, for the blessings in my life, and for the loved ones by my side. I see the light of God as a curtain of wisdom and support pouring all the love over us.

The journey is open to those in search and only those who see and feel the call for truth will embark on the journey into happiness and greatness—greatness for the good of all.

Stop judging. Instead, embrace one another and become one in mind, body, and spirit. Live from your heart and experience the wisdom of the light through your eyes, the eyes of the self.

Every morning, as the day starts, close your eyes and sit in silence. Experience the self. Savor the juice of life through the peace and love within yourself. Feel the joy within you.

Always look beyond the sky of the mind and ego. Then you'll be able to attain enlightenment and see the truth of life as it's meant to be lived—with love, happiness, and joy in your heart.

Be grateful every day, be joyful for what life presents to you. These are gifts of life for you to evolve and experience the wisdom of the self. The knowingness of your true self.

Through the eyes of my soul, my heart, I can see the reality and humanity of the self that is reflected in every ray of light, in every expression of creation, and every being of life. I rejoice in the vastness of life that is offering me all sorts of gifts to enjoy. I love to bathe in your wisdom and grow from it.

How wonderful and magnificent life is when seen through the eyes of self. Immerse yourself in the mystery and wisdom of the self. Go deep and enjoy the wonders within you. Recognize your infinite wisdom and divine qualities. Share these qualities in every encounter, on every breath, and with every step you take. Erase the clouds from your sight that don't allow you to see the light or let you experience the truth.

Jump in and enjoy the beauty within and the joy that pervades you!

Don't set conditions on anyone. Simply be with and enjoy the other souls alongside you in the journey. Only show sympathy for those taking the journey with you. We are all equals and evolving for greatness of the self.

TWENTY

THE DECAY OF LIFE

Hi! Welcome to my life, Masters of the Truth of Love. Thank you for your presence. What is our topic tonight?

THE MASTERS SPEAK:

The decay of life.

Everything in life is in the process of transforming from one existence into another existence. As a human, aim to embrace the vulnerability of existence itself. You are born, you die, but what happens between point A and point B?

The processes that occur between birth and death are the journey of life, the process of evolution into another state of energy and out of matter. When this is understood from the perspective of matter, with the mind of a human being, you suffer. Suffering is a perception when life is seen from the perspective of limitation and loss.

How do we overcome our suffering associated with death? How do we manage our feelings about the eventual end of our material being?

By understanding the duality of the self. You are both matter and energy. The energy of the soul is ever present. Although matter fades away, you remain. What is occurring is a transformation into a new state or form of expression.

How do we connect this with the laws of the universe you taught us?

Transformation is initiated by cause and effect. The law of existence and the law of acceptance will help you manage your suffering associated with death.

Sleep is part of the experience of death—it is like a daily death. Every time you sleep, you go into nothing. You go into the eternal void of the now, where oneness, unity, and love coexist.

TWENTY-ONE

LOSS

Here I am again, ready to embrace your presence and teachings, Masters of Love. What do you want to discuss today?

THE MASTERS SPEAK:

The suffering of those who experience the death of a loved one. By aligning with the laws of existence and the method of simplicity, they'll be able to process and understand death. It is intrinsic to human life. Death is unavoidable. It will always occur. It is ongoing. All cells inside the human body are constantly splitting off to form new cells and then dying themselves.

Why do some children die at such an early age of their lives?

It's part of their process.

What process?

The cycle of life.

Do we choose these cycles?

Yes. By evolution. By purpose and mission. Once you have achieved the mission for that intended life, the intended evolution is attained.

Do we get more than one opportunity to fulfill a purpose or mission?

Yes. For the greatness of the soul.

One fulfilled purpose or mission is not enough for the soul?

Yes and no. As souls, you are connected to the collective and there is always an entanglement of energies between souls. They communicate and ask for assistance from other souls, which, even if they are fulfilled and content with their existence and have no further need to evolve themselves will put themselves in service of other souls. In this way, entangled souls can achieve evolution of the whole.

Humanity is composed of families, communities, and nations of souls with one purpose only: greatness, harmony, love, and peace.

Wow, Masters, this seems profound for me, as I haven't experienced death.

Yes, dear soul, we know. But when you do, you will be filled with hope and peace. You will comprehend the process and the reasons for your existence. You will transform states with ease!

Is there no pain, then, in the moment we depart the earth? Depart human life?

No. You're simply leaving a temple. It is with gratitude you shall depart. Even unconscious people leave with gratitude because their souls know it is time to change states—either because their mission was fulfilled or there is a need to assist another soul elsewhere in its evolution and learning.

Who is in charge of this perfect system of recycling of souls and families of souls?

The inner qualities and power of each soul. Together souls create a collective force of intelligence that is able to create and recreate again and again. The superior force that you humans call God is all the forces of souls working together in their different states of evolution. Creation is a matrix of energies complementing each other for the good of all. It is perfect balance, harmony, and oneness.

Life is precious. Life is all. You exist to experience opposites, complements, master yourself, and expand into the greatness of the true self. Enjoy the process!

TWENTY-TWO

SEPARATION

Here I am, Masters. I'm open to your guidance, presence, and love! What topic do you want to explore today?

THE MASTERS SPEAK:

Separation.

What kind of separation?

Your separation from the true self—the self of oneness—that is empowered by love and the laws of existence.

The suffering in life starts when you disconnect from the primordial energy of the true self. By placing more weight on the needs of the body and ego than on the soul, you misalign with the true self and disorder begins. Disorder begins within your cells, tissues, organs, and psyche. You start to misunderstand your intrinsic, dynamic processes. Chaos in mind, body, and heart unfolds from there.

What can we do to heal the separation?

Breathe, be silent, feel the self within you, which is the super consciousness of eternal peace and connected to all. When you understand that you are one with everything else and that all is entangled in the matrix, in consciousness itself, you will live in flow. Allow your boundless essence, your divine consciousness, to be in charge of your existence and, life will become effortless and easy.

All is contained in the same matrix, in perfect correlation and balance for the good of all elements within it. The feedback within the matrix that perpetuates it is a back and forth movement of energies with only one goal, which is to expand and attain greater order.

There is an everlasting expansion and existence of matter.

What are the consequences of the separation of which you speak?

Disassociation from the true self. Disassociation from others. Disassociation from your purpose. Disassociation from life itself.

Separation brings pain and satisfaction at the same time. It offers you a temporary feeling of satisfaction. By hiding

KEYS TO LOVE AND HAPPINESS

how deep the discomfort in their heart is, people become numb. There is temporary relief in this. But that numbness starts the suffering that harms the mind, the body, and the heart. With separation, you become like a warrior fighting against your own happiness and purpose.

If you generate mental debris, in time it can degenerate into serious mental illness and even a deep desire to end your life. To separate from your body through suicide.

How can we deal with this in enough time to save lives?

By cultivating unconditional love, self-love, and practicing purposeful living. Will power also comes into play when confronting your desire for separation. Your will and desire to exist and live aligned with the true self has to be stronger than your sense of separation and suffering.

To attain a state of confidence in the now, try this practice. Place your attention and focus between your eyes and project your will to live and also the prospects of happiness, evolution, and oneness to the furthest reaches you can imagine. Holding this vision in mind brings peace and restores balance.

Ease is the natural state of the soul. From there, you flow into more complex patterns of existence and beingness.

Experiencing complexity in the order and information of the matrix leads to an evolution in consciousness. It is mathematically in order and flow. Creation is orderly complexity. The matrix of consciousness and creation is ever-existing and evolving.

What, specifically, can we do to get this experience of the order in the complexity of life?

Do breathing techniques and meditate. Use these activities to help you loosen up and trust. Surrender to the presence of the void of peace and complexity that has all the answers and information you need to be who you genuinely and naturally are.

TWENTY-THREE

SADNESS

THE MASTERS SPEAK:

How do human beings feel sadness? By means of the heart and limitations of the mind.

Through the lens of the mind, we translate sadness into tears. Tears are the drainage of the heart, helping to keep the heart light and at peace. They are a buffering medium so we may continue to be at ease with ourselves and our future experiences.

Crying is about releasing what doesn't serve you to leave a space for the feelings, emotions, and states that nourish your heart and emotional mind.

Is sadness necessary?

Yes, as a complement to joy and contentment. But in this sense, sadness is only a purpose, not an end. From this perspective, it becomes a transformative and evolving experience. It helps us grow, and this is what we are here for: to evolve into a greater self and form communities of eternal existence and evolution.

Very profound!

Yes, yes, it is profound wisdom for the soul who understands the qualities of the true self.

TWENTY-FOUR

TRAGEDY

My dear Masters, here I am trying to understand pain and sadness, when, in this moment, I feel gratitude, joy, peace, and ease. Only empathy and compassion help me understand something I'm not presently feeling inside. How beautiful it is to be able to feel for others when we are not experiencing that same emotion. But I embrace all. I'm ready.

THE MASTERS SPEAK:

Let's speak of tragedy.

What kind of tragedy?

Car accidents, plane crashes, and other tragic incidents.

What is relevant to know and understand about them?

That these are only ways in which the body, as matter, disconnects from the soul. There is no suffering in death. It is simply a change in the state of the matter. Tragedy is a catalyst for transformative processes in the matter of the body and its functions.

The true self or the individual soul can't experience pain because its state is eternal. The true self is composed of the ever-present energy of all the forces of creation combined. In the moment of a tragedy, there are only processes of transformation occurring to alter or transform matter into a new expression.

The ones who remain are perceiving the process of death as painful and suffering because they are seeing it through the lens of the bounded mind and the physical human experience of life.

If we humans are born to experience life in a body and to sense and live with a variety of different emotions and feelings so we may evolve from them and become enlightened, isn't the best way to grow from tragedy to immerse ourselves in its sensations?

Yes, but your suffering may be reduced by the understanding that every emotion is temporary. Aim always to view tragic experiences from the perspective of the heart, not according to the limitations of the mind. You are here for something greater than pain and suffering, even if you're not able to see it in a particular moment because your sight is clouded by emotion.

When you are upset or in suffering, breathe. Breathe and trust. Find as much ease as you can and use practices to calm your nerves. Remember that your true essence is light. Your true self is wisdom. You are higher knowledge and love.

Do your best to maintain peace and equanimity regardless of what is happening around you.

TWENTY-FIVE

SICKNESS

THE MASTERS SPEAK:

Sickness and disorder in the cells really is a condition of the mind and created by thought alone.

The frequency of a thought sends a chemical signal to the cell. A positive, nourishing thought creates order and balance in the cellular functions, which results in coherence and harmony of the whole being of a person at a greater level. The energy of one healthy cell radiates to the cells around it.

How an individual cell responds to the frequency of a given thought ultimately brings either order or disorder to it. The response is based on electrical charges that the thought, as energy, brings to the outer surface of the cell. Polarities create order and similarities in the charges create disorder.

As the thinker of your thoughts, you have to be aware of the nature of the thoughts you have. Negative thoughts are low in frequency. Positive thoughts are higher in frequency. Maintaining present-moment consciousness can play a key role in helping you create frequencies of thought that create order within the structure of your cells.

The cell is always a neutral receptor, and the mind—through its subconscious and conscious thought processes—is the leader or arbiter of which chemicals are released into the bloodstream that will bond with the cell.

Sickness is a collection of individual disorders happening at the cellular level. As groups of cells form into tissues and organs, and these join together in systems that are the whole "machinery" of the body, the body is made healthy or unhealthy.

You can prevent cell damage by changing your thoughts. This takes courage. For the mind must be stronger than the ego.

Remember, sickness only happens in the body. The true self is always working to achieve your greatest good, order, and balance—even when you feel sick or are damaged.

Go back to that silent space of stillness within, to that space of easiness, order, and peace where all the components of your system are in balance and harmony and can express their potentiality and the true self will help to restore your health to the degree it can.

What laws apply to healing sickness?

The law of the now and the law of order and reorder.

Sickness is a misalignment in the components of the cell, of the body and the self. This misalignment is due to the environment or the mind. The person with their thoughts that create order or disorder in the cell, will generate what you call sickness.

The cell has been created and set in the intrinsicality of your bodies to work as a perfect machinery of life, of expression and development. It is its nature, then the self with its mind and ego can disrupt the original intrinsic nature of order, balance, harmony, and potentiality of the cell.

How?

Driven by the need of the mind with its thoughts as frequencies that carry electrical charges (positive + and negative -) and the desire of the ego to express its control of the expression of the reality of the self.

And?

Here is when the recognition of the true essence of the self and the commitment to the principles that sustain life is a key to define the outcome in the body—either to express order and balance seen as wellbeing and health or disorder and disharmony expressed as sickness.

Then who is the commander of this process of the expression of life as order or disorder, as in the form of sickness?

The mind is the creator of the thoughts, either positive or negative, that will send a signal (through neurochemicals and the hormonal system of the body) which interacts with the outer field of the cell.

The cell is originally charged with both expressions of energy, the positive (+) and the negative (-). So, as the positive electrical charge of a harmonious, positive thought interacts with the field around the cell, the outcome will be order, because opposite charges attract and generate an electromagnetic field of order and harmony.

By contrast, if the thought brings a negative expression of itself with a negative charge as it interacts with the negative charge of the cell, the cell will repel it and produce a field of disorder, transmitted to the inside of the cell. Then the cell's entire process of expressing life and ways to produce energy will be distorted. This ultimately will translate into degradation of the cell as well as to poor efficiency in the processes of the cell and body. This extrapolates to the tissues, organs, and different systems of the body, which are formed by cells.

It's not clear to me the charges of the cells and the charges of the thoughts and their interaction. Because the thought (either positive or negative) will always encounter positive and negative charges in the cells. What happens when the thought gets in contact with the cell and finds both charges? What happens with the charge in the cell that is not interacting?

The charge in the cell is defined by what thoughts prevail, the positive or negative. Depending on this, a thought will be expressed as sickness or balance and order.

How can I explain this more scientifically please?

Leave it at the level of the subtle energy of the heart.

TWENTY-SIX

JUDGMENT

Shall I ask questions, Masters, or will you guide me?

THE MASTERS SPEAK:

Breathe and look around you. What do you see?

I see stillness, flow, harmony, peace, and order. I see greatness and balance. I see beauty and harmony.

That is what you, as a divine being, must choose to see every day of your existence.

Try only to see the good, the vastness, and the order in creation and the frequency of your thoughts will align easily with the laws of existence and the principles of nature. This will help you attain peace and balance as you undergo soulful expansion.

Enjoy the stillness within you and the beauty and perfection around you. Then glory and love will reign in your life.

Now, let's talk about judgment. Judgment is the seed of the ego wanting to grow and pervade. When we judge, we are simply seeing another through the dark lens of the ego's eyes. Judgment enables the ego to feel empowered and superior to others. The act of mentally stripping others of their qualities, talents, and gifts is the ego's way of feeding its need for satisfaction and victory.

We all are our true selves (souls) as well as our bodies and minds, which include our egos. If one of us is identifying mostly with our body, we judge because we are not able to see our divine qualities. We live in a limited reality, where we don't see beyond the confines of the mind in this case.

What natural law can help us overcome judgments?

The law of existence, the law of acceptance, and the law of investing.

When someone judges you, do your best to see the duality in that person and understand that separation is the perspective from which that individual is judging you—as opposed to oneness. This may give you greater acceptance and empathy for them.

Overcoming judgment, prejudice, and intolerance of people's differences resides in understanding your nature, which is dual. Acknowledging the natural divinity in others makes it easier.

Ultimately, balance, order, harmony, and love will prevail and pervade everything. This is the ultimate goal of existence.

TWENTY-SEVEN

EGOTISM

Thank you, Divine Masters, for the opportunity to serve you and humankind. What is our topic tonight?

THE MASTERS SPEAK:

Egotism. Egotism is the force of "lackness" and the desire of the mind to "not give away." Egotistical people have stifled any desire to use their gifts and talents for the good of others. There is a disconnection in them from their abilities and the qualities of the heart. As they don't identify with the wise and loving self within them, they are not able to give these gifts. That is why they keep them to themselves.

The opposite approach is to acknowledge your inner qualities and gifts and express them simply because your heart and soul naturally want to share them. It is the essence of consciousness to recreate itself through the act of expressing its potential.

What natural laws are the antidotes for egotism?

The law of giving. The law of receiving. Also, the law of love.

Egotism signifies an attempt by the ego to be in power, in control, and in total domain over the body. But real shifts in the heart and expansion of the soul bringing them into alignment with the magnificent light of the source of all that resides within you neutralizes the ego. That's why the world is growing in love and in consciousness.

TWENTY-EIGHT

GRIEF

THE MASTERS SPEAK:

When you grieve, immerse yourself in the pain in your heart and then awaken from it. Awaken from it with gratitude and love, with joy and peace, and with the intention to give and love, and to evolve and continue your path to greatness.

Yes, we know grief hurts and that it is felt all the way down to your cells. But also, it is a transformative experience. You can and will grow from it.

I have always believed that hope is the opposite of grief. If energy is dual, as you say, how may we know hope without experiencing grief? Is it possible to experience grief without suffering?

Evolution is a result of outgrowing the dualities of the self. If not for duality, life would not be life, and you wouldn't be yourself.

You could not be enlightened if you were not experiencing all the potentials of life—its complementary forms and shapes, such as love and pain, joy and sadness, abundance and lack.

The more joyful and harmonious aspect will always prevail over and supersede the challenging and disharmonious one.

Aim to see life as a journey of experiences rather than as a challenge. Life is a series of processes that carry knowledge, wisdom, and codes of evolution into the greatness of the true self and love above all. If unity is found along the way, the journey will be more fun.

Wisdom comes from grief—but only for those who have learned to live from and through their hearts. Love fills in the sense of emptiness of the self when living aligned with the laws of existence and the true self.

TWENTY-NINE

CONFLICT

THE MASTERS SPEAK:

Conflict is a difference in frequencies, an opposition of forces. It is a sign of the controlling mind, or ego, wanting to show its power.

What dissolves conflict?

Love. Apply the law of love and law of acceptance. Putting your focus on the Divine and the pure qualities of the true self in the one with whom you are in conflict and in yourself—the love, compassion, joy, gratitude, and so forth—will dissipate the differences and the opposite forces.

Let the power of the true self be in charge and love will dissolve the conflict.

In conflict, breathe and breathe some more.

In moments of fear, disconnection, grief, and tragedy, breathe. Breathe into the deepest spaces of your body. This will calm you down and reconnect you with your potentialities. Your inner light will arise, and harmony will be attained.

It is simple to end conflict when seen from the heart and with the eyes of the true self. When an opponent is felt from the soul and with love.

Let's end fear. Let's keep love and peace as a collective force to move all and pervade all.

Hey! Love each other. Don't waste energy on the degradation of the whole self (body, mind, and soul) or on the need of the ego to show its "fake power"; only the mind guided and driven by love can act as a positive nourishing ego.

Watch out! Be aware of which self is in charge when you are disagreeing or fighting.

Simply close your eyes wherever you are. Breathe in light, breathe out love and peace. Spread the light like a dust of harmony and acceptance all over you and all around you. Then, disagreements or disruptions of energy will dissolve magically and unequivocally.

Open your heart and an ocean of blessings will appear before your eyes. You will have mountains of strength to be shared and lands of opportunities in which all may coexist and grow.

Thank you, Masters, for such an easy and powerful tool for the world.

Awaken to sacred geometry and order. Search for it. Search for it in nature and in meditation when your eyes are closed in stillness.

What does it have or what does it teach?

The essence and order of life and the divine forces. Sacred geometry underlies evolution and the complexity of existence in the form of majestic love and light.

Does it feel good in the body?

It reorders in every aspect of the self, so it can be felt as an adjustment or unfolding—but it's magnificent and majestic rather than uncomfortable. Sacred geometry is pure love in its essence and expression. It is limitless and eternal in the now. No human definition is possible, just surrender to it and trust.

When?

In silence, in stillness.

Breathe easily and focus on the pineal gland in the center of your head at the level of your eyes and trust.

Allow yourself to dissolve into nothingness.

Peace will come when you dissolve in trust into nothing— into the divine light of peace.

THIRTY

FEAR

THE MASTERS SPEAK:

Fear is a lack of love and hope. It is a force, an energy, that stops and paralyzes us. It hinders our expression of our potentiality.

Why fear?

Because, in its destructive aspect, the fear of being your true self prevents you from experiencing life as it truly is.

True reality is the perception of an experience as seen from the purity of the heart and the brilliance of the mind in alignment with the laws of existence. And without the cloudiness of the ego self with its need to measure, control and judge.

True reality is the life you experience when you are guided by your true self and connected to the gifts of your heart like self-love, compassion, gratitude, and bravery. This puts you in alignment with the laws of the universe. It's a flowing reality that is not defined by expectations based upon false, egoic needs.

Fear causes you to give away your power. Then you project your actions into nothing. You are constrained from moving forward by lack of intention and the desire or will to do anything. The inaction ultimately leads to frustration, low-self-esteem, and degradation of the self. Your evolution is interrupted. Without meaning and a focused intention, you have no purpose.

In its creative aspect, by contrast, fear can be a force that propels solutions and your advancement in the journey of evolution.

When is fear a constructively transformational force?

When you align with the potential, knowingness, and power of your soul. If you empower your self-guidance system, you can use the force of fear to help you move forward. In such a case, fear is evolutive. It's like a fast-forwarding button on a digital audio or video system, a force that propels you quickly forward for your greatest good even though if in that moment you cannot see it and you feel uncomfortable.

Wow!

Be fearful of your perverse mind and weak ego. Be fearless and welcoming to your true self and intuition. Your true self (or soul) knows the way of doing things to benefit you and everyone around you. It finds the answers to all your questions and leads you to the road of easiness and fulfillment of your truth and deep desires.

Fear nothing but your ego. It leads you to suffering and dissatisfaction, if you surrender to it, which ultimately broadens the gap to the realization of your various potentials.

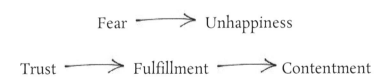

Fear ⟶ Unhappiness

Trust ⟶ Fulfillment ⟶ Contentment

Beautiful Masters, you are so wise.

THIRTY-ONE

MISUNDERSTANDINGS

It is an honor to meet with you again, Masters, and receive your wisdom and advanced knowledge for the good of all. Thank you for allowing me to be your vehicle.

What would you like to reveal today?

THE MASTERS SPEAK:

Misunderstandings.

There are different laws of creation at work here. The law of the now. The law of acceptance. The law of giving. When these three laws are not appropriately applied, there is misunderstanding and separation.

The law of the now works as a tool for letting go the differences between the beings who have a misunderstanding. Embrace the understanding that everything exists in the now. The truth for someone a moment before is the past; it no longer exists. So then, why would you expend energy on proving something you said that no longer exists. Let go and be in the now. Fulfillment, joy, peace, satisfaction, and ultimately, unity, exist only in the now.

The law of acceptance is applied here as a dissolver of opposite energies or points of view. A point of view is mental energy. By seeing the reality of the other as your own or feeling it as a possible reality within your heart, you will be able to bypass the limitations of the judgmental and egotistical person you are. All humans must contend with their egos. It is unavoidable.

The true self is able to feel and express sympathy. As it emerges, it dissolves differences and misunderstandings.

By simply doing your best to put yourself in the place of another, to "walk in their shoes," you're giving of yourself and your love and compassion. As simple as this is, it is how to apply the law of giving in the context of a misunderstanding.

Life is simple if it is lived from the heart and from the evolutionary wisdom within, which is the force of forward progression.

Anything else to share about misunderstandings?

See them as a chance to step forward in your evolutionary process into greatness. A misunderstanding is a chance to develop empathy and compassion.

You will be more compassionate if you release the mental need of your ego to prove its power and superior "knowledge." It's rightness.

True knowledge is nothing without the humbleness and wisdom of the heart.

Prove yourself to yourself, in your heart. Prove that you are expressing the qualities of the heart: gratitude, forgiveness, joy, love, equanimity, and compassion. Express these to yourself and experience them within first. Spend time within and acknowledge the greatness and beauty within, and then show and share your greatness and beauty with the world.

How privileged I feel to learn and live by these laws and the wisdom of your higher knowledge, Masters. Thanks for sharing it with me and the world. How else can I serve you today? Tell me, please!

Serve nature by breathing from her and breathing out your love to her.

Flow with easiness. There is nothing to prove, nothing to be or do but be and express love and wisdom from your heart. Stay focused and alert to the magic in the environment around you. It's always there for you when desired and requested from the heart.

Receive and give. Praise the good and beauty in the hearts of others. Be generous with yourself and others. Open yourself to the world and enjoy.

THIRTY-TWO

DELUSION

THE MASTERS SPEAK:

Delusion is a cloudiness of the mind in which the reality is altered. A disruption of feedback occurs. The outcome of it is separation. Separation of the self from its own truth and separation from those with whom we have interacted.

What hurts most in delusion is your perception of emptiness of the heart and of lack of sensibility and compassion in other people. The mind is always wanting to discern, analyze, and judge.

In a moment when you suspect you may be deluded because your mind feels foggy or you feel like the world is against you, do your best to become aware and get back in touch with reality.

Ask yourself:

- What am I feeling?

- And who is feeling this delusion? Is it the ego, the mind, the heart?
- Who feels betrayed? Is it the ego, the mind, the heart?
- Where in my body am I feeling this feeling? Which energy center?
- Am I processing this feeling (emotion) from the ego and the mind?

Once you realize which area of the self and of the body is affected by the delusion, it is important to recognize where the misalignment is located in your body. Is it in your abdomen or the area around your solar plexus? Is it in your heart or chest area? Is it in your throat chakra or neck area?

As you become aware of how and what you're feeling and where within yourself it is happening, you'll be able to identify that this feeling is not guided by your true self, which is pure. And that is not in alignment with your highest good.

Then, put your focus on your heart and breathe into and out of it for several breaths. Imagine it filling with light, and bring in an elevated emotion, like gratitude, and soak (rejoice) in it.

The purpose of this exercise is to shift your frequency to trust from victimization (or whatever it is that you're feeling). This will clear the clouds from your mind. This allows you to anchor in the true self.

Your authentic power emanates from the true self and your soul. This is your pure core.

What laws should we apply when we experience feelings of delusion?

The law of love and the law of the now.

Be curious about the potentialities of your self-expression. You are the weaver of the design of your life's tapestry. Stay aligned with the frequencies of elevated emotions, especially love, and do your best to be present in the now.

As you vibrate in oneness and joy, trust and truth, your delusions—whatever these may be—will fade away, dissipating like smoke in the wind.

THIRTY-THREE

AGONY

THE MASTERS SPEAK:

Agony is the feeling that comes from degradation of the self when living in the mind. It is the outcome of believing the dictates of the ego as a true reality and the only truth.

How does degradation manifest in us?

It manifests as despair, sickness, and hallucinations.

How can we heal agony?

Breathe into the deepest spaces in your body. Feel the light of oneness emanating from within you. Embrace all the forces and frequencies of order and balance, of the cosmos, of creation. Let the complexity and harmony of creation pervade your body and soul.

What law can we apply to come out of agony?

The law of existence and the law of love allow you to fill your heart with love and feel it so proudly within that order is restored, which alleviates the discomfort.

Embrace the beauty of nature and bring it to your heart as the voice of the Divine, calming you down and caressing your whole being. Listen and embrace the voice of perfection that sings from nature to heal your body and to nourish your heart with harmony, love, and the rhythm of creation with all its forces and frequencies.

THIRTY-FOUR

IMPERFECTION

Hi, Masters of Love and Happiness, I'm again at your disposal. My heart is open and filled with gratitude. Would you please define the "self" for me?

THE MASTERS SPEAK:

All the aspects of a being are the self, including the ever-present soul, the mind and body (the human expression), and what the human mind thinks the being is. This last is the ego.

Thank you. What do you intend to reveal now?

We wish to speak about imperfection.

Imperfection is the perception of the self and of what the self should be, as seen through the eyes of the mind, which have limited range. From within this bounded range of vision, you experience the self as limited.

As you transcend the limits of the mind and access higher realities of existence or higher consciousness, you are able to experience the self as a whole. Each human is part of the whole, which means you humans have no boundaries other than those defined by your minds.

Your true self is limitless. In its wholeness it encompasses all. There is no place for imperfection. There exist potentialities—different abilities to develop and express— within this infinite expression of the true self.

How does our belief in imperfection affect us and our relationships?

Belief in imperfection creates polarities in your experiences of self and others. There will always be a pattern or quality to compare to, such as good and bad, short and long, happy and sad, which leads to separation rather than unity and oneness.

What laws do we apply to shift our perceptions of imperfection?

The law of existence and the law of love.

THIRTY-FIVE

THE PATH TO MAXIMUM
POTENTIAL

THE MASTERS SPEAK:

The path to the maximum potential and greatness of the self is evolution. Although evolution includes everything in existence—and everything is continuously changing—only those understanding their true essence and the duality of the self will search for expansion. Personal evolution may be accelerated by opening your mind and your heart.

Focus your mind on the desires of your heart. The best way to manifest is to trust in the higher support you receive from us and from the forces of creation.

THIRTY-SIX

SELF-CULTIVATION

THE MASTERS SPEAK:

Inspiration is the pivotal force for those searching for expansion and greatness, love and happiness.

Cultivate yourself to be a presence of sympathy, easiness, and silent wisdom. These qualities will be felt and appreciated by those around you and related to you. Shine within yourself and spread this energy with smiles and acceptance.

We are one.

THIRTY-SEVEN

DISHARMONY

THE MASTERS SPEAK:

Disharmony is a force of unfulfillment within that is expressed as a form of conflict with others. It starts within when the self is not satisfied, and you do not feel whole. You then express dissatisfaction with others and the environment around you.

The experience of disharmony within is one of judgment, discontentment, and disapproval. Since others are reflections of what you feel within, that is what you will also experience in your life. If you feel disharmonious inside, you will experience discomfort, conflict, lack of acceptance, and disharmony around you too.

What laws of creation can mend disharmony?

The law of acceptance. The law of love. And the law of investing in the self.

Disharmony within the individual is the seed of conflict and destruction in relations of beings, communities, and nations. Actions that heal disharmony are expressions of self-love and love for others.

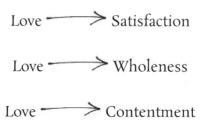

Love ⟶ Satisfaction

Love ⟶ Wholeness

Love ⟶ Contentment

Satisfaction, wholeness, and contentment restore harmony and balance in individuals, communities, and nations. Love is a transcendent force. It is an energy that promotes unity and oneness.

What more is there to know that will help us to evolve?

Let your heart be stronger than your ego. Don't label yourself by the roles and status of the ego. Instead, measure your value by the love and commitment you express for yourself and others, for your desire to do good, for your evolution, for wisdom that serves the good of all, and for increasing your comprehension of the true meaning of existence.

This is a beautiful mission, Masters.

Attune your personal energy with the energy of the true self. Live from the qualities of the heart, so that the frequency of your expression generates harmony within you and around you. As you do, this energy expands throughout the world and creates harmonious communities and nations.

THIRTY-EIGHT

LIBERATION

THE MASTERS SPEAK:

Detach yourselves from the ego, which is your fake identity. Release any need you may feel to "be someone" with labels, since you are already a divine being and significant in the eyes of God and the consciousness of creation.

You're a perfect being with qualities of infinite power and complexity. Enjoy these and flow through life with what you were born with: a pure self of boundless expressions and possibilities in existence.

Break your bonds with whatever limits you and makes you unhappy, such as the frequencies of unworthiness, self-judgment, and suffering. Expand yourself to the full reaches of the grandiose vastness of creation, as that is what you really are. You are limitless existence. That is the true self.

Identify with the true self and you will accelerate your evolution.

Detach from any need to prove yourself to others or to live out the expectations of others. Be free within and bond to your own truth and to the essence of limitless possibilities with your current reality. Reality is constantly evolving.

As you detach and relax, trusting your life to the hands of God and divine love, you will enjoy the freedom of flowing with the forces of creation, which only want to offer you fulfillment.

Life is magnificent and has everything to offer you for your greatest happiness. Bathe yourself in the gifts of creation. Align with the forces of order, expansion, and balance. Embrace everything in your life. Your heart has an inner impulse to evolve. Understand also that it is your right to be whole, loved, and happy.

Yes, Masters, I can see that it is our right to feel worthy and be aligned, to receive and give, to feel whole and enjoy our oneness.

Yes dear, it is as simple as that. Magic unfolds for those who believe in their divine and limitless essence. It's there for all to experience.

Any special message today?

Breathe, be at ease, and always look around. What do you see? Whatever you see is the reflection of what you are inside, so that's your best mirror in which to check your state.

Be beautiful, and you'll see beauty. Be love and you'll see love. Be truth and you'll see truth. Be whole and you'll see wholeness. Be magnificent and you'll see abundance all around you. You'll be in awe.

I love this message, Masters. Everything starts within!

Yes, and goes out as a natural process. So be conscious of what you are and feel because it will be reflected around you.

THIRTY-NINE

UNITY

THE MASTERS SPEAK:

As we experience self-love, the desire for unity awakens in us. Love is the underlying consciousness and frequency of unity. When the shared frequency of all the components of a reality is love, unity unfolds.

Is there a method with which to promote unity among my students, loved ones, and friends?

Put people in circles and tell them to place their attention on their hearts and to feel love, sympathy, compassion, and gratitude with a deep intention for ten minutes. All the people will get pulled together by a higher force of union. Love is like a magnet.

At the end, the group will function like one person.

If you were to extrapolate this method and use it among a broader community of people, imagine the unity you would get.

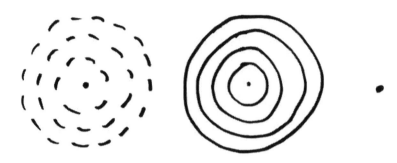

This is the goal, right?

One of them.

What are the other goals?

Balance, coherence, and happiness, which, in addition to unity, create oneness.

The ultimate, most important goal is to become one with all and the Divine in the eternity of the now.

FORTY

CONSCIOUSNESS

Hi, Divine Masters of Love and Happiness! As you know, I'm meditating four times daily these days at the retreat. and I feel more open to your presence than ever. Do you want to share a message with me tonight?

THE MASTERS SPEAK:

Yes, dear, we know what you're doing. We like it a lot.

A collective expansion of consciousness. That's what we see for you. Communities of love in expansion, in evolution, growing in their understanding of your essence and inner potentials.

What is higher consciousness?

Higher consciousness is a collective force that is all and exists in all and for all. At the level of consciousness, all is real and exists in its purest form. Consciousness is eternity in the now. It's where everything is born and dies at the same instant. It's a continuous process of existence in only one moment and in all the moments recurring in the now of eternity.

Consciousness is within every one of you, as it's the essence from which you came to exist. You exist in the now, and you will always exist as an everlasting phenomenon in the now of eternity.

Yes, existence in the ever-present now is infinite. However, this is the perspective of the now from outside of space-time where your bodies exist. Once you have no body anymore, you can be whatever you choose to be out of the possibilities that exist in the boundless realm of eternity. All is possible and approachable in oneness, as there is no duality. There is no separation and only unity in the now of the ever-present existence.

FORTY-ONE

REMINISCENCE

Reminiscence. *I love the feeling that this word gives me.*

THE MASTERS SPEAK:

Yes, reminiscing is the heart rejoicing in what gives it a sense of love, joy, freedom, connection, and belonging.

Reminisce about the shared moments of living from your heart, of the opportunities you've had to be in communion with your loved ones. It's like seeing a movie of moments you were in presence and it will help you to understand the joy of being in your heart in connection with others.

Don't reminisce about guilt or hatred, as you will raise those frequencies in yourself.

Only reminisce about love, joy, gratitude, and laughter.

FORTY-TWO

SYNCHRONICITY

THE MASTERS SPEAK:

Synchronicities are actions correlated with a cause.

The cause is a precious intention in the realm of consciousness that eventually manifests as a reality of profound surprise and joy.

Synchronicities have always been asked for, desired, even though they seem to lack causes. You manifest from the time-space dimension (the field of infinite possibilities) with thoughts as frequencies, but your third dimension is in space-time, where you see the physical manifestation of your desires.

Synchronicities can be miracles. When your trust in your desire is full, it will manifest as a transformative event. As a new reality that brings you fulfillment, happiness, wholeness, and alignment with the essence of the Divine. Your nature is to function as cocreators of infinite possibilities.

Synchronicity is one of the ways that the Universe speaks to you.

Be playful. Be joyous. Be grateful for the gifts of life.

FORTY-THREE

ENJOYMENT

Good morning, my beloved Masters! What's on our agenda today?

THE MASTERS SPEAK:

Enjoyment.

Wow, I like this!

Enjoyment is an energy that should be shared collectively by the people in the communities of love and nations of evolution and greatness that are emerging.

How do we cultivate enjoyment?

Go to your heart space and feel your true essence. From there, sense and acknowledge the beauty and greatness of being alive. Connect and be grateful for your gifts and talents. Enjoy them and rejoice in the simple beauty of being who you truly are.

And then share it. Sprinkle this energy like divine fairy dust all around you. Celebrate love. Celebrate fulfillments of heartfelt desires and outcomes that bring happiness to you and others.

That is true enjoyment. It's internal, felt in the heart and lived from the heart. It's not related to the external world or material life but to the joy of being content and fulfilled with who you are. Give of yourself.

What else, Masters?

As you celebrate life, remember to celebrate in harmony with your body. Keep a balance and always search for the joy of the collective.

Celebrate victories of the heart and the achievement of evolutionary goals. Celebrate the meaning of a purposeful life.

What is a purposeful life?

Living with the understanding of your divine nature. Life is purposeful if you apply that greatness to the evolution and happiness of the collective.

When you are connected to your heart and embodying the energy of love, you will express the simplicity of being.

FORTY-FOUR

ACKNOWLEDGMENT

THE MASTERS SPEAK:

Acknowledgment is a seed of understanding of what a being or an event is in its spiritual essence. It is to see the underlying reality behind any story and align with that.

Acknowledgment acts as a cohesive force between energy. When you acknowledge people's inner qualities, you are recognizing the true essence within them. This helps them add value to the expression of the collective.

When you appreciate and value the good within you, you can more easily see and recognize the good in other people.

The acknowledgment of good and pure actions is precious and constructive, whereas acknowledgment of the actions of the ego is destructive. They feed into the desire of the ego to prove its strength.

Acknowledge selfless work, self-expansion, gifts given from the heart, altruism, growth, harmony, and true beingness. And teach your children to do the same, so that they will seek fulfillment inwardly. Searching outwardly for fulfillment causes suffering and dissatisfaction.

FORTY-FIVE

FREEDOM

What is freedom?

THE MASTERS SPEAK:

Freedom is peace in beingness: to be in harmony within yourself and enjoy your gifts when they are used to promote your wholeness and the good of others.

Freedom is being boundless in the beingness of the self.

Freedom is having no limits on loving yourself and others.

Freedom is open expression of your potentiality and delighting in the process.

Freedom is to feel empowered from within because you carry the true treasure, your own true self into life. Freedom is not dependent on material possessions (or has little to do with material possessions).

Without freedom of the heart, life is stressful and demanding. It feels like a prison. Be free in your heart and open in your mind and use your body wisely.

Love yourself. Free yourself from the desire for external approval.

Approve of yourself by asking:

- Am I loving myself enough?
- Does this act bring me freedom and joy?
- Does this desire bring me expansion of existence?
- Does this thought or decision or action feel good and comfortable in my body?

If the answers are yes, then be free to be, to share, to give, and to receive in that way.

Releasing yourself from the chains of the ego gives you freedom. Start cutting it off. Liberate yourself of the trap of a fake identity and wanting things that bring separation and suffering.

Ask yourself:

- What do I show of me today?
- What do I give today?

Be a sympathetic presence. Do your best to put yourself in the place of the other, either to enjoy their victories or their discomfort. And keep looking for the truth of the self beneath the surface.

FORTY-SIX

ALTRUISM

What do you want to share with us today?

THE MASTERS SPEAK:

Altruism is a force of profound love and devotion wherein you put the ego aside and serve others with no expectations, doing things for them merely for the joy of it, seeking only love, peace, unity, wholeness, and happiness of the whole.

The energy of altruism has a frequency that illuminates the soul of those who feel for others and for whom the act of giving is natural. They experience profound joy without a need for recognition.

Altruists give unconditionally and fearlessly, simply because their nature calls for it. It's such a true quality for them that giving is effortless. There is no waste of energy.

How do we teach altruism?

By developing compassion and sympathy. Altruism will awaken then.

Is there a daily routine or practice to cultivate altruism within us?

To be compassionate first with yourself. Imagine what you would like to be or receive that would help you feel more whole, complete, purposeful, and fulfilled. Identifying your own needs will help you understand the needs of others. Do your best to fulfill needs that you can see.

FORTY-SEVEN

FLOW

Divine Masters, I greet you with love from my beautiful, sacred home on Margarita Island. Welcome. Thanks for pouring your light, love, and presence over this magical place.

THE MASTERS SPEAK:

Breathe in light, breathe out peace. Energize yourself with the grace of the Divine.

What do you want to reveal and teach today?

Flow. It is to exist and move from the potential that you are. Flow is your presence as energy moving and interacting with its own intrinsic nature and all the forces around you.

Flow is like the movement of particles of a phenomenon that exists only in the now. It only exists when consciousness is placed and intended over it.

Every now only exists in the will of a person as a desire—a desire with unlimited potential to manifest and be in the boundless existence of eternity.

If you understand that flow is a current everlasting potential of existence in every now, you'll be determined to want to evolve as a phenomenon of expansion in every now with your desires as a form of thought.

Thought is a frequency that carries information to be expressed in the limitless potential of eternity in the now.

Stay in the now.

Stay in the now.

Every time you sense yourself mentally wandering in the past or future, come back to the now, as we taught you. Place your awareness between your eyes and project the frequency, as an intention, into the energy field of eternity.

Being present in the now brings heartfelt fulfillment. The rest of your mental activity is an illusion. The mind is seeking temporary satisfaction for the senses and the ego.

When there is entanglement of various thought frequencies, the flow of energy you generate with your mind is massive and powerful. If this reaches a sufficiently high level of potentiality, the energy expresses itself as a collectively experienced phenomenon in the now.

There is a constant movement of energy through every now. Although each now is impermanent, the sum of all the phenomena from the independent nows is flow.

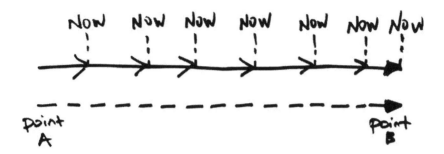

Eternity is one. It is individual moments and all moments combined.

Flow is constant. Energy is constantly moving. We see energy and we are energy. It's only energy here.

Would it be possible for me to see you, Masters?

You have sensed our energy.

Yes, but I want to see you as energy. Please!

No dear. Trust us, you will see us beautifully, and know it is us when you do.

What else is there to know about flow?

Flow like the wind. Flow easily and effortlessly into all and with all. This will bring easiness and love to your heart. Take the energies as winds of expansion into your evolution as a divine self.

If the wind feels good on your skin, rather than harsh, run with it. If the wind feels uncomfortable to the point that it causes you pain or threatens your existence, acknowledge it and let it pass over you. Wait for another wind that resonates with your inner potential of good and simply embrace it and move with it.

Flow with what resonates with your heart.

And how do we know that something is resonant?

You close your eyes, go to your heart, and breathe. Feel from that space. Test the frequency of the energy there. If it feels easy, joyful, expansive, harmonious, and aligned with your deep desires for greatness, then embrace it and go for it, fearlessly and trusting.

Thanks. That seems like an easy way for us to trust the energy. What more, Masters?

From the heart, enjoy all with acceptance and union—the plants, the ocean. Be generous and loving with yourself and all—you're all one. Feel them, thank them, and embrace them in your life.

I will! Thank you.

FORTY-EIGHT

THE SONG OF THE SOUL

Divine Masters, I am at your will to serve the world. What is in your consciousness to share?

THE MASTERS SPEAK:

Amuse yourselves with the melody of nature and the loving sound of your hearts. Orchestrate melodies out of cohesive frequencies of emotion, like love, sympathy, harmony, compassion, and unity. Be your own composer, creating harmonious notes that resonate with the true self, your soul. Write your own partitures and play your melodies in the realm of consciousness.

Let the whole enjoy your compositions as a gift. Delight the collective with harmonious notes that elevate the soul.

The silence of the heart can sing louder than the voices of all the human egos combined. Open yourself to the voice of nature as it carries the wisdom of the Divine and the notes of all frequencies of creation. Allow its boundless possibility to nourish your heart.

Recognize the voice of the Divine in every bird call, in every exclamation of the stones that knocking one against another amid the sound of waves crashing on the shore. There is boundless information in the sounds of nature that can help you evolve. Nature is at your service.

Breathe in pure air, exhale love and peace.

See with the eyes of the soul and the mind of your heart.

FORTY-NINE

THE WISE VOICE WITHIN

A fresh new day. A chance for love and joy. A chance to give and receive the blessings of life. To serve you, Masters, with all of myself and my love and gratitude. What is your message today?

THE MASTERS SPEAK:

Transform your life and you'll see greatness.

Move silently into the vastness and majesty of your being. Allow the voice of humility within you to be the loudest voice you hear. Your silent being is powerful yet delicate, and also wise.

The beats of a loving heart resonate as far as the forces of creation can reach. So, let love loom large in your heart and be your voice.

There is no need to convince anyone of your point of views. In the garden of life, every truth is like a flower and its essence (its color) is an individual expression. The garden is more glorious because of an abundance of colors.

Be generous with your smiles and good intentions. Be glorious in your self-expression. Be victorious with the blessings you receive.

Celebrate the magnificence of life and the beauty and uniqueness of every expression of creation. Cultivate the qualities of your true self.

Finally, practice being in the now daily. Developing this skill will help you achieve happiness and reduce your suffering. Please embrace this one simple suggestion. Make the practice your own.

FIFTY

DISAPPOINTMENT

Beautiful, loving Masters, I know I have to flow with what is now, but I was rejected from a job I wanted, and I feel frustrated. What advice can you give me about disappointment?

THE MASTERS SPEAK:

Dear, where do you feel the disappointment? In your mind or in your heart?

I am processing it in my mind, but I desired the position with my heart.

Remember, every now is a new now, another opportunity to develop your potential. Trust in the divine flow of things. Everything serves a purpose that feeds into the cultivation of the true self's greatness. There is always something more evolved for every individual to do who wants to give. According to the law of expansion, everything always moves forward.

Trust us, dear. We're on your path with you. The secret of simplicity as an approach to life is knowledge that deserves to be shared and understood. Live by it now.

Yes, I know, Masters, this is what I want to give the world. I've been asking for this for so long. And here is an opportunity to practice simplicity—a chance to walk my talk. Thanks.

Love and magic await you.
Inhale peace, exhale wisdom.
Inhale peace, exhale harmony.
Trust dear, in the divine forces and you'll receive guidance for your path. Make the law of acceptance yours.

FIFTY-ONE

HARMONY

THE MASTERS SPEAK:

Harmony is being aligned within and with all. Being at ease with who you are and how you live produces harmony. It is a peaceful state of being. Breathing is easy and comfortable when you are in harmony. Everything seems to be effortless.

Harmony on a broader scale is alignment of the being in every now of existence. The true self always has harmony at this scale. For the individual, alignment comes from accepting every now as the only moment in which to be and live. Harmony is available to those who are present.

Harmony starts from within. If you experience it yourself first, then you can share it. It is cohesive.

When there is harmony within, you can shape communities of love and peace. So, let the voice of the Divine whisper in your ear: "Be at ease, be at peace," and surrender to the sensations of harmony in your body.

Harmony precedes peace, peace precedes unity, and unity precedes communities of love. Communities of love create nations of greatness.

Relax into the simplicity of life.

Set the intention to be at peace.

FIFTY-TWO

EVOLUTION

THE MASTERS SPEAK:

Keep evolving into a more loving, openhearted, wiser self. Evolution is the fruit that comes from planting the seed of fulfillment and satisfaction.

Help others evolve by being a presence of knowledge, by simply listening to their hearts' desires. Also, by sharing your gifts with them.

Evolution is the constant flow of things seeking to reach their full potential.

What if our evolution stops for a moment?

Because of the law of expansion, you will always start growing again sooner or later. Eventually everything evolves into something more complex, intelligent, organized, and whole.

The ultimate goal of evolution is oneness. Many people are not conscious of their inherent oneness. Each of us has to heal and evolve to understand that we're part of the whole.

FIFTY-THREE

BEINGNESS

THE MASTERS SPEAK:

Beingness is the state of being in the now. Existing in the self.

The true self is limitless because it is oneness. Consciousness is limitless. Although the human body is limited by its boundaries, something of the true self inhabits it and enables you to experience oneness consciously.

Embrace your potentiality and see how far you can go in your beingness with the various qualities you embody as a human.

True beingness is lived through the mind and the heart as well as the body. The mind commands with its thoughts and the heart executes with its boundless love and truth. The body is where you experience life.

Remember, your heart is your powerhouse when it comes to manifestation because it has access to the Divine.

The triad of your being is the Divine, the mind, and the heart. There is no failure in beingness when existing from within this triad.

Existence can be all, or it can be nothing. It is eternal. It can be visible, and it can be invisible. Only the eyes of the Divine experience the oneness of everything that exists or has the potential to exist. Be true to your heart and you'll have access to your true nature. Bathe yourself in the ocean of love and present your divine qualities to the world.

Which qualities are divine?

Love, generosity, wholeness, peace, joy, light, oneness.

FIFTY-FOUR

PROCRASTINATION

Good morning, Divine Masters . My burning question today is this: How do we humans get caught up in procrastination?

THE MASTERS SPEAK:

Through lack of will. Those who procrastinate are not sufficiently committed to attaining their potential to impel them to act and override fear and self-doubt.

Procrastination leads to dissatisfaction and guilt.

Don't allow yourself to be imprisoned in the jail of a habit of procrastination and live with the torment of your mind judging you. Avoid getting stuck in an everlasting loop of negative feelings about yourself by cultivating your will to do things. Practice replacing negative thoughts with positive thoughts and encouraging yourself with loving acknowledgments of your worth. Utilize the qualities of your heart and your mind to overcome anything contributing to procrastination.

Let your will to expand and be at peace be stronger than any laziness or weaknesses of your mind that would get in the way of you succeeding in exploring your potentiality. Move towards your greatness incrementally if you must but keep going.

Align your mind and body with your vision of your goal and do not hesitate to fulfill your desire for this outcome. Celebrate the steps you achieve along the way. Open yourself to the changes that occur.

Every now is unpredictable. Release stress and anxiety. Relax and trust. Every time you feel overwhelmed, stop and breathe.

Breathe in peace, breathe out trust.

FIFTY-FIVE

DIVINE LOVE

THE MASTERS SPEAK:

Divine love is the supreme force and presence. It embraces us all, masters as well as humans. It fills everything in existence with love and peace. You may partake of it by accessing your purest nature from your heart. It is wisdom within and intention without failure.

By this we mean, when there is an intention from the divine self and the heart, there's no mistake since it is true to the being and supported by the laws of existence. It's pure and intended from the heart.

Divine love encompasses all creation. Its essence is of the purest nature. The only way to experience it is in the silence within your soul. If you sit very still and are quiet, then you may enter a state of grace where all you feel is peace, flow, and bliss. The grace is a taste of oneness. When divine love graces you, you can perceive that there is no separation, only love.

Divine love is infinite. All qualities of the Divine are boundless in their essence.

What can we do to cultivate divine love on a daily basis?

Every day, take time to experience your divine self. Travel within to the silence of the soul and simply rest there. Be as nothing. Rest in the eternal now.

Free yourself from your mind and body by immersing yourself in a vast ocean of eternal peace and oneness.

How can I be a divine presence for others today?

By being the qualities of the Divine. Be. Be forgiveness. Be humble. Be. Be compassion. Be. Be magnificent in your grace. Open your heart and see the true self behind the masks people wear.

Any other message?

Life is about understanding your humanity from the heart and expressing your divine self.

FIFTY-SIX

DETACHMENT

THE MASTERS SPEAK:

Detachment is a release into the true self and the vastness of existence. It is freedom. It is losing yourself in the Divine and giving yourself up to the simplicity of existence.

To be detached is to be internally free and feel at peace no matter what happens around you. It is a process or event of surrendering to the essence of the self in trust.

Detachment also is being who you are without masking yourself. This lack of ego is significant. It is important to detach yourself from the roles you play in your life and the false identities you create to play them.

Walk barefoot in the forest of life and let the sweetness of nature embrace you. No money, no material luxury, no social power can rival having peace in your heart. Detach yourself from the chains of any false identities associated with money, luxury, or standing and you will attain freedom.

You may have these things, but you must aim to be internally detached from them.

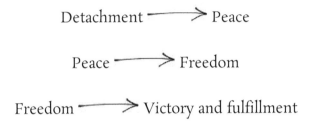

Detachment ———→ Peace

Peace ———→ Freedom

Freedom ———→ Victory and fulfillment

The victory of being our true self is the greatness of existence.

FIFTY-SEVEN

REINCARNATION

Dear Masters, is there such as thing as reincarnation?

THE MASTERS SPEAK:

Yes. Rebirth is the start of a new life or existence in the now of vast possibilities to be. As the matter of one human body decays there is a reordering of its energy to manifest again. The true self reshapes itself so it may continue its evolution and expansion toward oneness.

Without death and rebirth there would be no evolution. Evolution is a process of intrinsic ordering and reordering of forms into something more evolved.

How beautiful it is for your soul to have a chance to live again and again. Each time you are reborn, there is a new chance for you to be a greater self than in your previous existence.

Where this gets interesting is that every time you beautiful beings wake up after a peaceful night's sleep you are also reborn as a new self into a new now of existence. Take this opportunity to be aware of which qualities you want to embody, cultivate, and share. Throughout the day, be conscious and purposeful with the new self you are exposing to others and the world.

Be for the world around you and the world around you will be for you as you are. Breathe and be. There's no need to do and do and do. Just be. Be a vehicle of oneness and conscious living of unity and love.

So, what do you want to have and see around in your life? If you want joy, be joyful. Generosity? Be generous. Love? Love yourself. Forgiveness? Forgive yourself. Good? Be good to yourself. Abundance? Be abundant in all the virtues of the self and the qualities of the heart which bring true richness and vastness. Harmony? Be at peace with yourself. Acceptance? Accept and love yourself first, as you are.

FIFTY-EIGHT

THE TRUTH OF YOUR EXISTENCE

Divine Masters, I embrace your presence and I am ready to receive your messages with gratitude. What do you want to reveal to me?

THE MASTERS SPEAK:

The truth of your own existence.

Wow! Yes, please do! What is that truth?

That you are light and love. Live from that truth, it's a divine statement. You've prepared yourself to evolve and be with knowledge and deep desire. You had a longing for giving love and wisdom and the manifestation is now done for you.

Yes, and I feel so pleased and grateful to be living with a purpose. Purposeful living!

Your energy is bigger and more powerful than what you may know. Every morning, with your eyes closed, from your heart say:

"I am love, and this love is for all.

"I am light, and my light ignites everyone.

"I am a living force, and my energy is propelling everything forward.

"I am giving myself in devotion, for love and greatness.

"It is, it will be, it is."

Speak these affirmative words of everyday magic and your creativity will unfold. This will help you evolve into a presence contributing to the expansion and awakening of humankind.

This is wonderful. Thanks for this tool. May I share it?

Yes, with the ones you feel are ready and evolving in their consciousness. Share it with those with open hearts. They should speak these words every morning, too.

FIFTY-NINE

THE RECYCLING OF PARTS

THE MASTERS SPEAK:

Observe the movement of all things, being and living. Observe how each thing has an inner power, and how its forces are in alignment with the forces of creation. Everything is in motion!

It is important for you to understand the movement and recycling of all parts of existence. This will help you to move with the cycles. You have your own internal cycles of reordering or reshape yourself into something new for every now. Please accept and understand that change and movement must occur to all energy forms.

Each human is energy in motion in the eternity of existence.

Please embrace the changes in your life. Do not resist the movement and reshaping of things in your life—or you will suffer because of it. Everything needs to evolve in the realm of true existence, and true existence is limitless, everlasting, ever existing, and oneness.

Also please accept losses as new beginnings for others and for you. They are undergoing the transformation of their energy into something new. You as well. When you experience a loss, your reality reshapes too.

Even if your loss hurts, embrace it. Possess the frequency of grief temporarily and then release it. Let the suffering go. Understand that everything and all is sustained in perfect balance and order, even if, at moments, it doesn't seem to be. There's always a temporary disorder involved in the shifting of evolution and moving into a new now in existence.

If you understand this, you will alleviate your suffering.

Bathe in its wisdom waters of life and drain waste that doesn't nurture and serve you. Drain old habits. Drain old thoughts. This is how to change your beliefs and recycle yourself in every now.

What else can we do to move and recycle our energy?

Move the energy of your body by doing what the body was created for; move it by moving. This is according to the perfect order and limitless intelligence of God. Enjoy the perfect machinery you possess. Be love and light in motion.

Movement = change

Change ⟶ New manifestation of matter and
energy in a new now

Be love in movement.
Be light in motion.
Be knowledge in evolution.
Be oneness in unison.

SIXTY

SINGULARITY

THE MASTERS SPEAK:

A singularity is the simplest expression of energy shifting into the totality of existence in the now. *Gravitational singularity* is a term used in physics to define the particle as an expression of matter under compression as it falls into a black hole.

How does viewing ourselves as singularities serve us in our lives?

You're matter as an expression of energy condensed in a body. Your body's unique self-expression is a spark of the energy of all in existence. It's part of the infinite expression of life in material form existing in a tiny expression of energy, like the atom.

As beings of energy, humans are complex expressions. But you are simple too. Together, you exist as a whole group of energy expressing itself like a single one. Individuals are correlated to one another.

How does this idea of humans being singularities impact our daily lives? How do we apply this information for the good of all?

Be as complex and as simple as the most basic expression of the self, which is the pure self. The true self is both a source and a receiver. It is a vessel that holds all expressions of life, including you.

Let simplicity be your prayer—the core tenet of your faith. Use simplicity as your medium for relating to others. The simplest way to be is authentic.

Accept your uniqueness and move forward in all things from that state of being. Understand and embrace the fact that your being is all there is, and you have nothing to seek outside you. Just discover yourself and embrace its genuine essence to exist with ease and comfort in your own expression of creation.

Be as simple as a breath, be as effortless as the blink of an eye, be as inclusive of your nature and as exclusive of your nonreality in the now. By this we mean don't try to make anything yours that does not feel aligned with your inner truth, true self, or heart as a reality. In other words, don't accept anything as true that doesn't resonate with you.

Existence is simple if you understand that everything you need to be and evolve to be is already within you and that you have potentiality. It's housed in your body and mind, in the magnificent potential that you embody.

When you want to remind yourself to be simple, close your eyes and give yourself a moment to breathe in silence. Enjoy the peace within and spread the frequency to every cell in your body. Be peaceful in your heart. Do not come out of that state regardless of what surrounds you. Remember to reconnect with yourself anytime you would like to feel grounded in peace and higher knowledge.

Be in charge of your existence in every now. Embrace only the experiences that give you freedom of the heart, leave you in peace, and bring a joyful feeling of fulfillment for achieving a happier, more evolved self.

Embrace harmony in your relationships. Do not prove who you are or what you align with in regard to knowledge. Do not allow your ego to possess you. Instead, possess your heart and listen to your higher self.

SIXTY-ONE

SYMPATHY AND CONNECTEDNESS

Divine Masters, what would you like to show or reveal today?

THE MASTERS SPEAK:

Sympathy and connectedness.

Why these two qualities together?

Because one leads to the other. If you don't feel sympathy, fellow feeling for another being, then there is no connection.

Sympathy resides in the hearts of those wanting to give and receive. In the web of human relations, everything is interconnected. What you are, you receive back from life. What you ask for, you receive. In the moment you feel sympathy for yourself, you start to feel worthy of receiving.

Now the connection you have with others is a matrix in which to relate.

Connectedness with others starts within. When you are connected to your heart, and living according to its guidance, you are ready to give. The qualities of your being serve a purpose in the lives of others—they complement their qualities of being.

There is an everlasting correlation in nature, a continuous sharing of forces creating balance for all the living beings supporting one another in existence—which means *coexisting*. If you understood the power that your own existence has over the existence of others, you would become more conscious and your actions would change.

Change must begin inside you. Your thoughts create a reality not only for you but also for others, because your thoughts dictate the actions you choose to take.

From our perspective, the connectedness in the matrix of existence is self-evident. It is necessary for you to raise your consciousness to a level where you can plainly see this too.

Feel genuine love for yourself and you will love others. Caress yourselves with thoughts of expansion and goodness, and you will begin to see a reality around you that nourishes you and others within it. If the actions you take are aligned with the laws of existence, you will experience order, expansion, unity, happiness, and fulfillment.

Can you see now how connectedness creates a broader and more powerful and stable force of order, balance, and harmony?

On a daily basis, do your best to simply be aware of how your presence and energy, expressed in the form of thoughts, emotions, and actions, generate a reality for you and for everyone immediately involved with you.

The ultimate goal of your existence is oneness, and this can only be achieved and experienced through connection. The origin is knowing your inner relationship with the source of all being and all that comes from it.

Every human carries this same energy intrinsically. This energy is shared and experienced as a whole in the matrix of existence. This is oneness.

SIXTY-TWO

THE GRANDEUR OF THE HEART

Divine Masters of Truth, thank you for your presence with us.

THE MASTERS SPEAK:

We are grateful for your dedication and commitment.

We wish to share knowledge tonight of the grandeur and power of the heart. Through the wisdom of the heart, you can achieve abiding happiness. Always center your awareness in your heart, regardless of any experience you are currently immersed in or any scene you are passing through. The outcome of this choice will bring you satisfaction and fulfillment.

Measure the greatness of others only from your heart, knowing that what you are measuring are, in fact, your own qualities and worth. The worth of the self is immeasurable.

How do we center our awareness in the heart?

Simply close your eyes and go to the heart, feel your way there. By default, you will start to feel gratitude, love, self-love, joy, and a desire to stay there. If you think of each of the qualities of the heart with the intention to sense them and live them, then you can spread them throughout the world and the cosmos like a dust of light and love. By doing so, you will be raising the vibration of creation and contributing to oneness.

Sleep is also important for your heart. Sleep is a medium for rebalancing and reshaping your physical system and it is a chance for your soul to bathe in the purity of divine love and unbounded presence.

Treat yourself well with a good sleep daily!

SIXTY-THREE

EASE

THE MASTERS SPEAK:

Ease is an effortless flow of energy that is in alignment with the laws of existence. Ease brings peace and harmony, so embrace life with easiness. Let the winds of wisdom caress your heart and the sounds of nature guide your path.

Be easy in your manner of living. Be easy in how you relate to yourself. Be easy and accepting of events that occur in your life. Be easy in understanding your own mistakes and weaknesses.

Ease can be disrupted by dissatisfaction. Do not put this unnecessary weight on your heart. The heart is pure in its essence, so suffering does not fit there. Only the ego suffers and feels dissatisfaction. But the heart is untouched by ego, so you won't suffer if you live from your heart!

It's important for you to recognize where, in your being, discomfort, dissatisfaction, and pain are being experienced—if they are. If the source of discomfort is your mind, it's because you're living either in the past or in the future. Ease is always occurring in the present. Choose to live in an easy manner, where you relate to yourself and others from a heartfelt, sacred space of purity.

How do you want to live, with ease or with dissatisfaction? The ego will choose the negative path while the heart will choose love, empathy, unity, expansion, and harmony.

Let your heart's desire to be at peace and happy be stronger than your mind's egoic demands. Heart wisdom is weightless. Ego is heavy. Be wise in identifying what does not belong to the true self. Be simple. Feel.

In certain moments, you will be called to apply what you know at a deeper level of your beingness. Choose to do that which resonates with your heart and your deep desire to love, evolve, and do good. Listen to the voice of the Divine within you.

This will simplify your being and doing.

To create easiness of being in every moment when you feel vulnerable, close your eyes.

Breathe in light, and exhale peace.

Breathe in love and exhale harmony.

Inhale the light of the source, and exhale calmness.

Remember, living consciously means using higher knowledge and inner wisdom to be so happy and satisfied with yourself that you can be open and relate happily with others.

Dear, be easy and conscious in every now. Sometimes life shows you something you don't expect or desire. This is a chance for you to choose, Will you experience inner peace and satisfaction or disharmony and victimization?

Breathe. Breathe and be aware. There is greatness, balance, peace, and love around you.

SIXTY-FOUR

COMMUNITIES OF LOVE

THE MASTERS SPEAK:

We wish to speak to you today about communities of love. Such a community is a collective for conscious living whose philosophy is based on sharing only the qualities of the heart, for the good of all in the community, and knowing the impact that will be made all around the circle of love.

Creating a community of love starts with practicing self-love and self-forgiveness, reconnecting with your heart and dropping the ego. This enables you to feel how worthy you are of receiving the grace of the Divine and everything wonderful that creation has in store for you.

Explore your potentiality within your community of love and it will help you to discover which gifts give you the most fulfillment when you share them.

Duality is an intrinsic quality of your human aspect. Embrace the complementary expressions of energy in your existence. This will enable you to form and maintain relationships based on sympathy, empathy, and inclusiveness!

Be conscious of what sustains your life, and take care of it: the oceans, soils, animals, plants, and air. Acknowledge that these are all part of the cycle of life that your community of love inhabits.

Continue evolving your consciousness through practices that cultivate the potential of your higher self, like conscious breathing, meditation, contemplation, selfless giving, silence, and stillness.

As you grow into a more conscious being and you feel fulfilled within, bring your self-satisfaction, self-love, peace, worthiness, and inner harmony to the purposeful living of your community of love. This will help you to expand and share them.

A community of love can be as small as a family and as big as a country. It's associative and inclusive and always growing. It will take you from an individual experience of selfless living to a collective experience of fulfillment. Communities of love unify people and give them a place to share victories and mutually rejoice in each member's fulfillment. People can expand together. Members love unconditionally with no roles, no status, no masks of the ego self.

Harmonious living in communities of love is what will bring oneness to your world.

SIXTY-FIVE

INSPIRATION

My loving and amazing Divine Masters of Love and Happiness, I'm so happy to encounter you again and receive your higher knowledge. What would you like to discuss?

THE MASTERS SPEAK:

Inspiration.

Being an inspiration means showering a fountain of blessings over every person with whom you interact. It means sharing your gifts and insights for the evolution of others without needing recognition, praise, approval, or gratitude. Inspire simply by being your greatest self and guided by the voice of your heart and brilliance of your mind.

You can inspire yourself by cultivating the qualities of the heart and serving yourself and others for evolution, love, and greatness.

Inspiration ⟶ Motivation

Inspiration ⟶ Movement

Inspiration ⟶ Expansion

Inspiration ⟶ Satisfaction

Inspiration ⟶ Synergy

Inspiration ⟶ Harmony

Inspiration ⟶ Collective growth

Inspiration ⟶ Heartfelt celebration

Inspiration ⟶ Joy

I love this, Masters. It's a clear and simple prescription for living.

Yes, easy knowledge to understand and live by.
Only the wise, humble ones who embody their true essence inspire.

SIXTY-SIX

MAGIC

THE MASTERS SPEAK:

Magic is effortless living that's aligned with the laws of existence. Then, all the forces conspire for your beingness, doingness, and evolution.

How may we enjoy that magic?

When you feel worthy of receiving the blessings of life, you will experience magic. Trust your intrinsic connection with the Divine and the forces of the universe.

Experiencing magic means you have understood your limitless nature and acknowledge your birthright to create limitlessly. Rejoice in the manifestation of your desires.

Move through your life with acceptance, easiness, trust, and connection and all the forces that sustain creation will create magic for you.

Here is a practice that will enable you to see magic.

Every morning or now in the day, close your eyes and breathe with awareness into your whole self: mind, body, and soul.

When you feel centered and aligned, visualize and sense that you are inhaling the light of the Divine.

Then, inhale all the energies and forces that sustain life.

Think of a desire in your heart. Just sense it and leave it there. From your heart, release it to the divine intelligence with profound trust. Spread it like a dust of love and trust.

Enjoy the manifestation of your desire in your heart as a reality.

End the practice by expressing sincere, profound gratitude for the manifestation of your heartfelt desire.

Feel worthy. Feel complete.

As you go about your day pay attention for signs of magic.

Is magic available to everybody?

Of course, dear! Magic is your birthright.

Start showering in the cosmic dust of magic that the

Divine is constantly pouring over you. See it, sense it, and enjoy it. This magic—the grace—is there for you to rejoice in.

SIXTY-SEVEN

ENLIGHTENMENT

Divine Masters of Love and Happiness, I am here before you to embrace your presence, guidance, and higher knowledge. What do you want to reveal?

THE MASTERS SPEAK:

Let us speak of enlightenment, the greatest expansion of the self in its evolutionary journey.

Being enlightened means being able to acknowledge your weaknesses and being willing to overcome them from the heart. It means evolving as a being in true connection with yourself and everything that makes your existence possible.

Approach the experiences of your life as opportunities to prove to yourself the greatness of your heart and the brilliance of your mind. Make the best choices you can to establish a true connection with your most divine essence, as this is your real nature and origin.

Ignore temptations that would nurture your egoic self. Go for the choices that help you grow in spirit. Free yourself of the chains of self-judgment and disapproval. Remember, the self's natural tendency is to expand further into greatness—to explore its potential.

Enlightenment comes from being simple in your approach to everything. If you have understood your divine qualities, regardless of your human characteristics, you will evolve.

Enlightened people live the truth of the heart and the wisdom of the true self (soul).

How do we achieve enlightenment?

Cultivate the qualities of the heart. Be truthful in your beingness.

Devote yourself to a life of connection, sympathy, and unity where your freedom of being emanates from the simplicity of your expression and the grandeur of expressing your true self. Elevate yourself above the limitations of your mind and ego. Also detach yourself from the chains of addiction and from any need to define everything and everyone based on your own reality and expectations.

Employ practices known to cultivate self-knowledge, inner silence, and alignment of the body, mind, and spirit. Enlightenment ultimately leads to oneness.

SIXTY-EIGHT

COUNTERBALANCE

THE MASTERS SPEAK:

Counterbalance is a buffering tool for you to use when you intend to balance yourself. If balance doesn't work, counterbalance by default.

How does it work?

Having an opposite force is what gives something balance. Although it would seem to create disorder momentarily, it generates syntropy.

Can you give me a clear practical example?

Yes! In a situation where you feel distressed or out of balance emotionally, especially if you have already tried to restore your balance, you can counterbalance by immersing yourself more deeply in the situation or experience. Perhaps you have tried a self-help technique or set an intention for balance. Through visualization—mental and emotional rehearsal—increase the effect of the variables that are causing your imbalance.

Internal intensification of your feelings will catalyze a return to order. This will be created by default. It is the intrinsic nature of the self and an aspect of the psychology of any living organism to restore its syntropy after an inner disruption.

In this case, where you have added intensification, the techniques of self-knowledge and inner peace will unequivocally work, and inner balance will be restored.

Counterbalance is a tool of consciousness. It only works when there is awareness of a need to apply it and an intention to be balanced.

Why is it important for us to learn this technique?

Because, for you to generate harmony and unity, there has to be balance within you and in your collectives. By any means necessary, you want balance to be experienced individually and collectively so you can live in oneness, which is the ultimate goal of existence.

KEYS TO LOVE AND HAPPINESS

Order $\longleftrightarrow$ Balance

Balance $\longrightarrow$ Satisfaction

Satisfaction $\longrightarrow$ Harmony

Harmony $\longrightarrow$ Peace

Peace $\longrightarrow$ Unity and love

Unity and love $\longrightarrow$ Oneness

SIXTY-NINE

COMPASSION

What is compassion, Masters?

THE MASTERS SPEAK:

A higher feeling of love either for yourself or for another.

To feel compassionate, you must first understand your own weaknesses. Then you will be able to feel and acknowledge the weaknesses of others as your own and feel genuine compassion for them. In the realm of true love and oneness, compassion simply unfolds as an essential gift or quality of the self.

Compassion is a generosity of spirit. It involves giving your gifts to embrace and heal the weaknesses and suffering of another. Compassion is love in action between beings.

Compassion is not seeing scarcity or sickness in others but seeing their inner potentials for goodness and wellbeing.

The evolutionary purpose of compassion is to form connections so you may grow in joyful mutuality.

If you knew how much simpler it is to be as one, you would avoid all the suffering, fighting, conflict, and hatred. The moment you accept the truth that you are sparks of the divine light and universal spirit of existence in the eternal now of creation, oneness will be shared among you all.

The truth may be found within you. In your divine true self.

SEVENTY

APOLOGIES

Good evening, Divine Masters of Higher Knowledge, I'm honored to be guided and loved by you. What is my duty tonight? How may I serve you and the world?

THE MASTERS SPEAK:

Apologies.

What about them?

Apologies are when the mind excuses itself to the ego self. The true self and heart do not need apologies since they are a living force of truth and love.

Please, be aware of who is demanding an apology. Is it your ego or the mind, which both feel a need to control, manipulate, and judge you and others.

Only apologize to your heart for not living from it, for not nourishing it with self-love and other feelings and emotions that increase your joy, balance, harmony, peace, expansion, and true fulfillment.

Apologies are the outcome of a non-heart-centered and unconscious existence.

Here is where the law of the now plays a key role. If you were aware of your existence only in the instant of creation that is the now, your choices, actions, and words would only bring you satisfaction, peace, harmony, and unity. Apologies would not be needed and would not exist.

You may need to apologize if you create separation from other people either by believing that you are more or less than them. Separation is created if you judge, control, victimize, manipulate, harm, or fight.

Please, live in your heart and do your best to cultivate love, self-love, generosity, unity, self-awareness, equanimity, sympathy, compassion, and gratitude so that you can live your life and relate through the qualities and aspects of the self that generate harmonious, peaceful, and loving relationships without separation. Then there is no need to apologize because you're living a truthful existence from your heart, which is a sacred space where happiness and fulfillment reside.

Masters, this is beautiful and inspiring. It's teaching me to be heart-centered and aware of where I live within myself: in my mind, my ego self, or in my heart.

Yes dear! That is what being aware of being aware of your existence is. Conscious living will contribute to the creation of the communities of love and oneness.

What else, Masters?

Apologize to no one but yourself—and only for not living in your heart and listening to the wisdom of your soul.

Instead, celebrate the victory of being your true essence— a divine self with a heart opened to love, to give, to receive, and to enjoy the fulfillment of living in alignment with your own divine roots and the laws of existence.

Inspire instead of apologizing.

Let's call apologies the voice of the hidden self (the ego), which wants to be seen and recognized as the true self, though it is actually only a facet of the whole self.

Be only your true self and you will experience self-love, peace, and harmony within yourself and in the world around you.

Thank you, Masters! As you reveal your higher knowledge to me, I become more conscious and more loving, heart-centered, and committed to my true self. I also feel more inspired to make a positive difference in the world and be a presence of love for everyone. I want to keep mastering myself until I become a supermaster of love.

Inhale light, exhale peace.
Inhale, exhale harmony.
Inhale love, exhale wisdom.
Inhale the dust of divine light, exhale oneness.
Inhale peace, peace will be.
Inhale your own light, greatness will be—and oneness will exist.

When do I use this breathing? To attain what state?

To center yourself and stay on your path to great fulfillment, oneness, and unity internally and externally. Use this breathing technique to enjoy an easy, effortless life where you are in alignment with the forces of creation.

And remember, live as simply as you breathe and blink your eyelids. The method of simplicity is very, very important for a happy life and oneness.

SEVENTY-ONE

PRESENT-MOMENT IMPULSES

Divine Masters of Truth, I am at your service for the greatest good and happiness of all. What do you want to reveal, show, or teach me and the world tonight?

THE MASTERS SPEAK:

The knowledge we share with you is extensive—profound and purposeful. It carries energetic codes necessary for higher evolution, love, and greatness of being. We are supporting you. We sustain the matrix of creation underlying everything that exists with our ever-present love and light. All is embracing all in the eternal void of existence.

When I am creating, how can I recognize what is there for me to use?

You'll feel an impulse that is superior to your limiting beliefs, and you'll follow your impulses naturally. That is part of all the magnificence and grandeur offered to you in this journey.

Live each now and surrender to each now with trust. Every now brings boundless extraordinary opportunities for you and the mission to make a difference in the world.

Thanks for holding me with such loving and wise presence, and for your guidance.

SEVENTY-TWO

CONSCIOUS LIVING

Divine Masters of Love and Happiness, I receive your light, love, and knowledge with much gratitude. Thanks! What do you want to show me today?

THE MASTERS SPEAK:

Every day, take time to travel within for at least one minute, two, three, or longer. Enjoy the peace present within the vastness of inner stillness. Let the voice of the Divine whisper the secrets of existence and the grandiosity of creation to your heart. Let the forces of creation caress your beings with their limitless order, coherence, and information.

Open your heart to the love that moves around you. Search in the eyes of each person you encounter for the truth beneath and love within. That is what you are made of: truth and love.

Obey your heart and follow the brilliance of your mind, as they will guide you to take the most fulfilling and enjoyable path of your evolution.

Enjoy the journey of a real, conscious life and you'll attract others to enjoy it with you. Gather in schools that teach the skills of self-knowledge where people can evolve without restriction. Create open spaces for the sharing of love and higher knowledge.

Share your gifts with the generosity of the Divine.

Breathing is life, and this life is for all. Loving is a right and this right is for all. Air and love are basic nourishments for the self. Bathe yourself in them daily. Then, go out, open your heart, and breathe in life, love, and order. Rejoice in the act of giving and receiving. Celebrate your own magnificence.

Embrace every now as the only instant in which it is possible to exist and manifest. Live by the law of the now.

SEVENTY-THREE

ONENESS

Divine beings of love and higher knowledge, I am so excited to meet with you again tonight. What do we need to understand about unity and what do we need to do to achieve it?

THE MASTERS SPEAK:

Oneness.

What is oneness?

Oneness is unity in every eternal now of existence. Oneness is all and nothing at the same time.

Why is it important to achieve oneness?

So that you are able to understand the origin and ultimate goal of existence itself. Oneness is all the forces of creation combined and working simultaneously in multiple nows of existence. It is every expression of a possible now eternally expressed in the infinity of existence.

Wow! As a human, it's hard to process this definition of oneness.

But it's a real definition, as it encompasses all the perceptions you experience as reality.

How do I teach the reality of oneness?

As both the origin and the end of existence in the now of eternity.

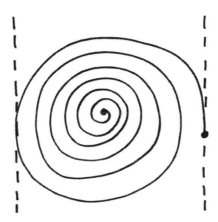

Oneness is everlasting existence in the now of eternity, expressed as multiple experiences of its own potentiality for existence. After oneness has been attained, you will be able to understand the origin of life and all the potentials that exist in the ocean of creation.

Remember. You are sustained by all the forces of the universe, each playing its role in your existence for the good of your essence and evolution.

SEVENTY-FOUR

TRANSITIONS

Here I am, Masters, ready to embrace your presence. What is in your consciousness today?

THE MASTERS SPEAK:

Transitions.

What are transitions in our lives?

The temporary experience of learning for a higher and more evolved knowledge in your lives.

Every step of your path serves a purpose in your evolution, so be conscious in every now, as it is a transition to the next new now in the evolution of your existence.

From the perspective of consciousness, growth and self-expansion take place through changes in the state of the energy—either when the energy is in the form of the boundless expression of consciousness itself or when it is in a material form. Everything is energy.

Let the movement of life follow its natural flow. All in creation is in flow and rebalancing itself for the purpose of oneness.

How do we align with the flow and rebalancing of creation?

By going to your heart and aligning with and acknowledging its voice. The voice of the heart knows and feels the forces of creation, since everything has the same nature. Everything is an expression of consciousness.

Close your eyes. Center yourself using conscious breathing. Then, from your heart, sense your connection to the energy of Mother Earth. Radiate your intrinsic energy— your inner light—to the far reaches of the universe, feeling everlasting bonding in your heart where you become the center of the bond of the infinite of the union. Feel communion with the whole of creation.

By doing so, you will attain unity with the synchronous flow of the forces of the universe. Experience their oneness, consciousness, divine order.

SEVENTY-FIVE

UNCONDITIONAL LOVE

Good morning, Divine Masters of Love and Happiness. What wisdom awaits me today?

THE MASTERS SPEAK:

Unconditional love and magic. You are the creator of your reality, dear, which you are creating with the vibrations of your heart.

Unconditional love is a moving force of wholeness that pervades all for the good of all. It is the acceptance of all the expressions of creation as unified, regardless of differences. At the level of energy, there is no duality or separation. All energy is contained and expressed, shared, and enjoyed in the entanglement of true bonding.

When you understand the intrinsic unity of creation, you will search for unconditional love naturally. Also, be defined by your true nature, which is divine consciousness.

Love is the energy that the heart recognizes as emotions or physical feelings. Heartfelt feelings and emotions create your current reality in every now of your existence.

Which feelings and emotions do you want to host in your heart? Which reality do you want to manifest? If you would like to experience an unconditionally loving reality, then host feelings and emotions of love, connectivity, expansion, limitless creation, unity, evolution, vitality, order, balance, and oneness. Intend to vibrate only feelings and emotions that take you to experience those states of fulfillment.

Live from your heart. The true magic of creation resides in its sacred space. It is the machinery with which you manifest new realities.

How do we cultivate unconditional love?

Through a daily practice.

Center yourself in your heart and breathe in and out from that space. Focus on your feelings of unity and connection with everything in creation. If you need to pick one focal points, such as someone or something you love, choose it to cultivate the sensations of connection. Radiate emotions you equate with experiences of connection as a light that bonds you with everything in creation.

Unconditional love will be experienced and understood through this practice. As feel your connection to all, you will sense that your nature as a being is the same as all the nature of everything else that exists within the matrix of higher consciousness.

Thanks, beautiful beings of love and higher knowledge!

Stay connected to your heart. You may trust that magic is available to you.

SEVENTY-SIX

AMBITION

Divine Masters of Love and Happiness, good morning. What is in your consciousness to share with me and the world today?

THE MASTERS SPEAK:

We wish to speak of ambition.

Ambitions are goals that the ego wants to achieve. They are not real to the true self, however. In the desire to achieve something, separation is created between the heart and the mind. Ambitions are like dreams in the sense that they are goals set by the mind to fulfill the intentions of the ego. But they are not real goals.

Are you saying that we have to learn to differentiate an ambition from a soulful goal?

KEYS TO LOVE AND HAPPINESS

Yes, please. If not, you will be trapped in a never-ending loop of illusion, searching for satisfaction.

A true goal comes from the desire of the soul to use its powers of creation and fulfill its potential. Driven by the heart, the higher purpose of a goal is fulfillment of any goal that is for the good of the self and the evolution of the self.

When you place all your heartfelt emotion into achieving a goal with a focused intention and work in the mind, soul and body, towards the fulfillment of it, you will achieve it gracefully and harmoniously. If a goal is not felt in your heart, it will never become a reality for you.

And, of course, an intention needs to be in alignment with the laws of the universe for its creation to be effortless and harmonious.

How may we discern that what we are pursuing is an ambition?

Through the feeling in your heart. If you feel peace, satisfaction, and wholeness in your heart, it is a goal. It is a true desire that will bring you inner fulfillment and evolution.

If you feel expectations and stress, it is an ambition. The goal is based on a fake need of the ego self, which is searching for the validation of its identity and recognition from the outside.

You will feel exhausted by pursuing such intentions as they are not in alignment with the laws of existence and the flow of life.

What else do we need to know about setting goals?

Always envision from the heart, feel from the heart, and live from your heart.

SEVENTY-SEVEN

INTEGRATION

Here I am, Divine Masters of Love and Happiness, ready to serve you and receive your guidance and wisdom. What do you want to show me today?

THE MASTERS SPEAK:

Breathe and give your cells pure air. Nourish them with life. They need balance and ease to exist.

Okay I did. It felt good and releasing. I feel nourished. What now is relevant for me to know?

Integration.

After you have experienced a reality and you understand its essence, you have processed the knowledge and/or expansion meant for you to learn and acquire from that reality. This realization of the changes you have experienced is *integration.*

Integration is the point when you are able to define changes in your state of being in a particular reality that you have experienced from different perspectives. Then you are able to go beyond, to expand your vision to encompass a broader, new reality. So, after every integration, immersing yourself in the next new reality will give you the chance to experience life from a different perspective.

This is what broadens your understanding of existence itself—your understanding of the connectivity between all that exists within the whole matrix of creation. Through integration, your evolution occurs. Integration helps you understand your relation to all.

Is there a daily practice for us to do to cultivate the habit of integration?

Yes, and it is indispensable for your expansion and journey of evolution.

Being aware, in every now, will enable you to be self-aware. There are moments in which you need to stop and acknowledge your state of being.

Ask: How am I living, how am I existing? How am I relating to others? how am I treating myself (body, mind, and soul)? Do I understand my current reality? From what perspective am I viewing and experiencing it?

Practicing being aware of your inner dynamics will develop and strengthen your ability and skill to integrate. Always ask yourselves those questions from the heart. Do not try to trick yourself. If you are not truthful, then all will be an illusion rather than a step forward in experiencing your greatness and oneness.

What else, Masters, about integration?

Please make it an activity of your daily life, so that growth, evolution, understanding of your origin and relation to all will be attained.

Be candid, be wise, be joyous. Trust your impulses. Listen to the voice of your heart and the wisdom of your soul. Laugh always. Vibrate in easiness and happiness.

SEVENTY-EIGHT

THE GLORY OF EXISTENCE

THE MASTERS SPEAK:

Glory is the most elevated state felt by those who live aligned with the laws of existence. It's a state in which emotions like unconditional love, satisfaction, peace, fulfillment, bliss, wholeness, and oneness pervade the whole self and guide its living.

The glory of existence is the maximum state in which you can immerse, experience, and enjoy your reality and accept every perspective of it as true and valid without judgment, victimization, and measurement or comparison. The glory of existence derives from the integration of all the processes and forces within the entire matrix of creation.

Masters, can we compare the glory of existence to the goal of attaining oneness?

When there is oneness, there is no duality. Comparisons don't have a place in oneness. Oneness is the goal of existence. It's a limitless state in constant flow in the matrix, where all exists and manifests in simultaneous and infinite realities.

I see, you mean it is boundless and nothing, and full.

Yes dear. Although from the confines of the human mind it's hard to grasp it in its entirety, that's basically how oneness is.

Please tell me more about glory. I want to be sure about the definition.

It's victory, the feeling of complete, infinite fulfillment that you get from experiencing universal consciousness, where everything is entangled and interwoven for the good, evolution, and existence of all.

It's also a state of celebration, filled with contentment and a blissful sense of wholeness.

Which is the practical aspect of glory for us to live by or know?

That glory of existence is understanding of your nature, your process of evolution, your connectivity to all that exists, and your expression of all your potential in each different reality you experience. It is the feeling of fulfillment of your greatness in the everlasting eternal now of existence itself.

Celebrate life, acknowledge life, and rejoice in the blessings of life.

SEVENTY-NINE

CORRELATION

What would you like to reveal and present today for the world to know?

THE MASTERS SPEAK:

Correlation.

What about correlation?

It's a mutual movement of energy that generates a continuous feedback, balance, expansion, and recreation of realities simultaneously in two beings. It's a constant feed of information for the energy to express as realities that complement each other.

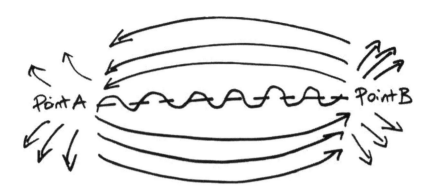

It's a sharing of energy in both directions, with a generation of a vibrational field of information that sustains the relation of both hearts. The energy shared feeds each of the potentials of reality to be expressed or manifested. That is how the beings of the field of creation relate to each other.

And how do I apply this concept in my own life, to my own self?

Visualize and know that you are a field of energy creating realities within and around your field in every now of your existence. You are that point A or point B at the same time, since there is a continuous feedback of energy defining both realities.

So, I visualize myself and sense my soul as a receiver and giver or a conductor of energy to generate realities?

Yes, through your thoughts as the wave of energy through the state of your inner biology (balance, order, rhythm, recycling, recreation), which is also expressed and shared between the fields.

Wow, Masters! Where do I take this concept?

To you and to everyone.

EIGHTY

SIMPLICITY

Here I am before you, Masters of Truth. How may I serve?

THE MASTERS SPEAK:

Life is simple, take it as it is presented to you. Be amazed and surprised by its complexity, magnificence, abundance, and order. The order makes life's different potentials accessible to you. Simplicity comes when you align with the flow of the forces of creation.

Follow life's rhythm by connecting to it with your heart. Feel from there, create from there, and live from there regardless of the constant movement and shifting of things around you. Stay connected to your presence, be aware of your reality, and embrace it with awareness.

Do not control, *flow*.

Do not resist, *allow*.

Do not judge, *embrace*.

Wow, this is a wise and beautiful message. Thank you.

This formula for simplicity is part of the secret of happiness. If you understand what living in your heart gives you, your journey to oneness will be easier, simpler, and faster.

Breathing is part of the simplicity of existence. Breathe in everything that nourishes your heart, replenishes your body, and enlightens your mind. Do not wait for things or realities to materialize, be them. What you are, you become.

EIGHTY-ONE

CLARITY AND MANIFESTATION

THE MASTERS SPEAK:

Let's speak of clarity and manifestation.

What about clarity? Clarity in our dreams, desires, thoughts, and goals?

Yes, dear. Clarity is the baseline to start your journey in every new reality, in every now.

Remember that you are the creator of each reality you experience. For that reality to be manifested as the reality you want it to be, you have to be clear and know which is the reality you want to live through. For this to be, you have to start with clarity in the desires, thoughts, and emotions that shape the manifestations of that particular, desired reality.

If there is no clarity in the origination of the reality you want to create, a defined reality will not be created for you.

So, how do we create a particular reality?

When there is alignment between a desire, specified as a goal, and your thoughts and emotions are vibrating at the same frequency of the desire, you will see the manifestation of the new reality. Only then.

When there is perfect alignment between a desire, thoughts, and deeply felt emotions, that "deep desire" will harmoniously manifest as the desired reality or outcome.

Manifestation starts with emotions that are driven through a thought to create a new reality.

When there is alignment in the frequency and vibration of the desire (emotion and thought), the reality will manifest effortlessly and harmoniously. It will manifest and exist in harmony with all of the forces that sustain life and that rule the flow of life within the matrix of universal consciousness.

How do we develop sufficient clarity in our daily lives for manifestation to occur?

Through different techniques that increase your self-awareness and create coherence, such as breathing exercises.

Try the following methods.

Conscious, heart-centered breathing. Sense yourself taking air into your heart space and exhaling from there.

Yoga and other forms of exercise. This improves the movement of energy in your body and balances the hormones in your endocrine system.

Hydration. Intake plenty of water.

Contact with nature. Exposing yourself to the sounds, colors, textures, and magnificence of nature will show you how simple, harmonious, limitless, balanced, and diverse life can be. You can emulate the properties of wild nature to reset, rebalance, recycle, bring order back to your life, and sense the purpose of your essence. Simply connecting barefoot to Mother Earth with the conscious intention to ground yourself and align and attune with the cycles and energy of nature can give you a sense of clarity, alignment, and sustainment.

Eating leafy green vegetables. These leaves are packed with vitamins, minerals, and fiber that reduce the risk of heart disease and high blood pressure and prevent mental decline. They provide a good amount of oxygen to the cells, including the neurons. This type of food can increase your mental clarity and overall function.

Meditation and contemplation. Through a regular practice of mediation and/or contemplation, you can achieve a state in which you release mental and emotional stress from your system. When you get into a state of restful awareness during meditation, your blood pressure regulates, your heart rate goes down, you release stress hormones, your breathing relaxes, your immune system is strengthened, and brain neurotransmitters are released. All these things will allow you to sleep better, increase your mental clarity and creativity, reduce inflammation, restore homeostasis in your physical system, and enhance your overall performance.

In addition, meditation and contemplation provide you with the chance to reconnect with your true essence and experience inner peace. This will help you to discover the infinite possibilities and unbound potential of your higher (divine) self. Therefore, you will become a healthier, happier, and more balanced being, which will translate for you into higher awareness and better knowingness of yourself.

Trusting in your divine consciousness. Your higher self is pure and unlimited in its essence and potential to create realities, so when you connect with this higher intelligence within you, you get a true vision and clear answers through your intuition, flashes of creativity, and certainty. Trust in this wise inner guidance.

Listening to your heart. Your heart is pure in its essence and expresses itself through gifts like self-love, compassion, love, gratitude, and joy. If you relate to us and to others of your own kind from the purity of your heart, your life can flow with more ease, harmony, meaning, and fulfillment.

Asking yourself this series of questions:

- What do I deeply desire?
- Will the achievement of this desire (goal) bring me joy and true fulfillment?
- When do I want this reality to manifest?
- Is my goal in alignment with the laws of existence that sustain the flow of life?
- If the answer to the preceding question was yes, then remind yourself of your desire, feel the sensation of its energy, and release it to the matrix of universal consciousness with trust that it is already done.
- Be that reality. And live by that reality. In the process of manifestation, you have to become that reality in the sense that you have to feel and sense it as if you already are living that reality. You do this with your thoughts and emotions.

Doubt and unworthiness are like fog in the sky; they will prevent you from seeing the reality in front of you. So, if you are feeling doubtful and/or unworthy, release these feelings. Then, empower yourself with clarity. Having clarity about your goals will give you a boost of confidence and worthiness.

You are worthy of inhabiting the reality you dream of and want to live in.

Feel worthy, act ("be") worthy, and you'll receive new realities.

Makes sense, Masters!

Dear, believe in yourself and trust in the divine order of existence. All is sustained in perfect order, balance, and correlation within the matrix of universal consciousness.

In this context, you have everything you need to be a presence of love. Be in charge of the reality you live in. Vibrate high in love, gratitude, worthiness, and joy. Live it and enjoy it.

EIGHTY-TWO

CONTRAST

THE MASTERS SPEAK:

In the midst of duality, contrast reveals opposite realities or opposite expressions within certain realities. At first, contrast is usually perceived as a split-off or separate meaning. But what contrast is actually showing is a range of potential expression.

Within any reality there are potentials. And this is where the grandiosity, complexity, and simplicity of life coexist.

Through the lens of the human mind, contrasts are seen and perceived as threats. In reality, contrasts are complementary.

How do we integrate and translate this understanding of contrast in our daily lives?

Beyond what your eyes can see, existence is a movement of complementary forces in constant flow, order, balance, and harmony. Existence is boundless and holds them all. If you can embrace this perspective, you will understand contrast in the true way, aligned with what it really is.

In existence without the confines of a mind or body, contrasts are complements entangled in an infinite expressions of different realities.

Furthermore, outside space-time (the material world you inhabit), there is nothing to measure.

Masters, is the message here for us to embrace differences?

Yes, dear, when you embrace contrast, harmony unfolds, unity unfolds, and oneness is attained. If you perceive a contrast, use it as a boost. Contrast can help you perceive your personal reality as more truly representative of you, and therefore, as more beautiful and meaningful to you. Let contrast be a force that inspires and impels you to believe in the reality you want to create.

Masters, please guide me to peace within and acceptance of this new reality.

You are peace and acceptance, dear. But you also have emotions that need to be felt, moved, and expressed. Then rebalance comes. That is your path.

EIGHTY-THREE

ABUNDANCE

I am here, Divine Masters, embracing your light, love, and higher knowledge. How may I serve you and humanity for the good of all today?

THE MASTERS SPEAK:

Abundance.

Abundance is the natural state and flow of life, of existence. Abundance is existence with all its potentials. It is the state of limitless expression. You do not need to create abundance, as it already is. It exists.

As a human, when you understand your origins and realize that you are part of the whole and entangled with everything that exists, you will *be* abundance since you have and hold every potential within you. You don't need to "create" abundance, you simply need to acknowledge and realize you are the potential embodiment of abundance.

Which conscious practice can we do for a state of abundance?

Close your eyes and start centering yourself by breathing from your heart. Deeply inhale. Easily exhale. Continue breathing like this until you feel grounded and calm. Breathe in divine light, breathe in celestial dust, breathe in all the forces and potentials of existence.

Feel and visualize all this energy as a river of infinite potential flowing through your entire body. Sense abundance as profuse flow of energy all over you. Sense and visualize how you are bathing yourself in all the potentials of existence. Bathe every cell, tissue, organ, thought, emotion, and feeling with the potential of abundance, of life, of possibilities.

Feel worthy. Receive it all. Take it in with gratitude and celebrate your abundance, your boundless existence, your limitless ability to create and manifest. Feel grateful, content, whole, and one with all. Soak yourself in the potential of abundance. Become it and express it. You are abundance. You will be, and you are.

Anything more about abundance?

Relate to everyone from your state of abundance, so you will generate more abundance in the world around you. Be magnificent and share your abundance in all aspects of your existence. Be a fountain of love and a river of joy. A wind of wisdom and a soil of greatness. Be love from your heart. Be wisdom from your soul. Be brilliance from your mind. Be life and give life.

Keep being love no matter what. Love is your essence.

EIGHTY-FOUR

ENTANGLEMENT

Divine Masters of Love and Happiness, I feel so honored for your presence and support for my journey to make a difference and raise the consciousness of humanity. What is relevant for me to see, know, and receive from you today?

THE MASTERS SPEAK:

We wish to speak of the entanglement of things.

What is entanglement?

It is the correlation and connection of every potential in a determined reality.

It is the sum of all the potentials of expression of a reality, coexisting at the same time (or now) with infinite realities.

Entanglement could also be defined as the experience of all forces of reality combined in a network of shared knowledge for the good of all that exists within the matrix of universal consciousness.

Why is it important for humans to understand entanglement?

Because, as sparks of universal consciousness, humans exist by the same principles and laws of existence as everything else in the matrix. You have access to the shared network of information in the form of thoughts and emotions. This feedback is indispensable for your existence!

Here is an illustration of entanglement.

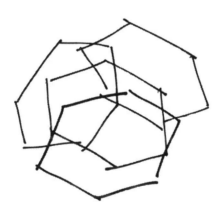

What do I do with this image?

Rotate it counterclockwise.

How far do I rotate it?

A quarter. And then rotate it two quarters clockwise.

More, Masters?

Turn over.

Upside down, you mean?

Yes.

What is this image, Masters? What is its purpose?

To show you entanglement in superimposed realities or potentials of existence. Its purpose is to illustrate their relationship to one another. The potentials are coexisting, interwoven, and networked. Entanglement generates balance, coherence, and singularity. Unity and oneness.

Entanglement is a natural process that is clearly expressed in many forms: in a spider web, in an artichoke, in a beehive, in a bird's nest.

I see, Masters! That is beautiful and illustrative!

Release yourself in the void of existence and you will create. Trust and live, trust and feel, give and receive, celebrate and rejoice.

EIGHTY-FIVE

OPPORTUNITY

THE MASTERS SPEAK:

Life is filled with potential for you to take part in and play with. Each now is an opportunity to exist—to be, to do, to give, to evolve.

Could we then say that an opportunity is equal to any now in our existence?

No, they are not the same. But opportunities unfold within each now as potentials if you are able to acknowledge and experience the potential. Then, the now becomes an opportunity.

Opportunities become opportunities only when you consciously want to create them out of a potential in the now of your existence.

So, what is our practical or evolutive approach to perceive more opportunities?

If you open yourself up to a state of worthiness and abundance, you will be able to see the potentials that exist around you in every now. Then, you will create a reality in which you are able to express and experience all the potentials that you are as a self.

What role do opportunities play in our lives?

Opportunities are there for you to experience, integrate, and evolve. This is part of the process of understanding and coming closer to greatness in your evolutionary process.

EIGHTY-SIX

THE VOID

Thank you, Masters, for bathing me with the energy of your light and pouring your love and higher knowledge through me for the good of all in the world. I am at your service!

THE MASTERS SPEAK:

The void is space in no time, which is infinite. where all exists in the nothingness of all possible realities and potentials, waiting to be experienced and realized.

It is the conjunction of all the forces in existence after they have expressed themselves already as all the potentials.

You can relate it to as an everlasting spiral of darkness in an emptiness of eternal peace in the nothingness of all possibilities of existence and creation.

How do we access the void, Masters?

Close your eyes.

Align yourself in mind, body, and spirit.

Then, release yourself to the universal consciousness and feel one with all. Become one with the whole in the eternal now of existence.

Stay there and lose yourself in nothing. The void of creation.

When you access the void, you will experience magic. You will access the knowledge of all that coexists within you. Forget who you are, become nothing. Be fearless and eager to discover your true essence and purpose in existence within the matrix of creation.

I have tried, Masters, but I still haven't experienced it as you describe it. I guess I have to surrender more and leave aside my fear of the unknown.

Yes, dear, we know you are a work in progress! You will realize it, you will attain.

Trust, there is only magnificent love holding you. The void is eternal peace in the nothing of everlasting knowledge and correlation. It is wonderful and beyond what your senses can perceive, realize, and take from.

Anything else we should know about the void, Masters?

Yes. Be generous with yourself and immerse yourself in the ocean of the inner silence. Dive into the infinite knowledge that resides within. Listen to the voice of your soul and follow the path of expansion into the eternal experience that pervades all in creation.

Open your pores and you will receive. Open your eyes and you will see beyond the confines of your sight.

Open your heart and you will experience true love and peace. Follow the guidance of your inner voice, of your soul, and you will access the realm of the whole.

The void is oneness.

EIGHTY-SEVEN

INTRINSIC ORDER

What is intrinsic order, Masters?

THE MASTERS SPEAK:

Intrinsic order is the arrangement of all the physical forms at the molecular level. This arrangement takes place on the scale of the cosmos and on the scale of the microcosmos. It all starts with the forces that entangle everything material that can be expressed in a molecule.

And?

What we want you to observe is the mirroring effect between everything that coexists in the realm of the all. The whole is mirrored in the smallest unit of condensed energy in matter.

Masters, what is your reason for sharing this information?

To enhance your understanding that matter, as an expression of energy, is arranged and ruled by the principles of subtle energy. Therefore, every layer of reality is a mirror of every other. This observation will help you understand how limitless you are. How infinite you are. You can flow as easily and effortlessly as the lightest and subtlest of forces, since that is at essence exactly what you are.

Observe this order in the arrangement of the cosmos, in the arrangement of the cells and atoms in your body, and in your thoughts. Let your thoughts be ordered, coherent, and aligned with all that surrounds them, and you will create harmonious outcomes.

Is there more to know about intrinsic order?

Only inner peace, exposure to the energy of nature, and understanding your inner potential can help you gain the full benefit of intrinsic order. Soak yourself in silence with the intention to reshape and reestablish your natural order at the molecular level. You will attain it. It will permeate all of you, including your heart, brain, and other organs. Your emotions and thoughts then will reorder, harmonize, align to the same purpose.

What are the practical aspect of this concept, Masters?

Always search for harmony, alignment, attunement, and coherence, and your life will flow effortlessly. As a being of energy, you are meant to flow.

EIGHTY-EIGHT

A FREQUENCY GLOSSARY

Divine Masters of Truth, at what frequency do you exist? How do you measure your frequency?

THE MASTERS SPEAK:

It is immeasurable by the human mind. It goes beyond your confined expression as beings of matter.

Yes, Masters, but how do you define or name it—the frequency at which you flow?

It is *kadeverious.*

Masters, to what frequency do you elevate me so that I can communicate with you?

To *unlicorious.* We raise your frequency closer to ours and become one.

I'm grateful for this gift. Masters, how else can I use this frequency? To have access to what? Or to feel or see what, specifically?

Dear, you may use it to communicate with us and with many other beings of light that are serving you to elevate the state and frequency of humanity.

So, Masters, lubridicious [a word channeled on a different occasion] *is different from kadeverious.*

Yes, dear. One is a state of our expression of energy and the other is a frequency.

And what is the difference between a state of energy and a frequency?

The state can be altered, the frequency is stable.

Do you mean you are vulnerable to change?

We are in constant order and reorder of energy for matters of fluidity and flow.

Okay. Anything else important for me to know about this, Masters? It's kind of hard for me to process this information. Why is that?

Because it is not understood through your parameters and dogmas.

From my perspective, I just flow with our connection and way of communication, which I call telepathy.

Yes, dear. But what matters is the convergence of our consciousness. Loosen up.

EIGHTY-NINE

SHIFTING

Here I am, Divine Masters, excited to meet with you again! I am open to receive.

THE MASTERS SPEAK:

You are shifting to a higher frequency.

How do I shift to a higher frequency, Masters?

By soaking yourself in water and experiencing the qualities of the water.

How often do you want me to submerge in the waters?

Now, by now. It is not about numbers. You'll see and feel it.

Okay. Any kind of water? Swimming pool or is ocean better?

It doesn't matter.

What should I do in the water?

Feel the movement of the water, be free, flow. Receive and bathe yourself in the flow of the water, in its wisdom and frequency of energy.

Why is it important for me to raise my frequency?

To receive higher codes and knowledge from us.

Sounds wonderful.

Deep inhale, easy exhale.
Deep inhale, easy exhale.

What do I give today?

Your light. Your heart. Your smile. Your vibrantly beautiful self. Be you and only that beautiful true self of yours. In truthfulness resides true beingness. Resides happiness and freedom.
Oliconarys.

What is oliconarys?

The state of the perfected ones.

Are there perfected ones in human existence?

No. Perfection is only experienced and attained after all your cycles of evolution when you become nothing again after being all.

I see, Masters! Is this definition or language the same in all higher realms or only in your dimension?

To all of us in these realms.

Why is it important for me to know about this state?

For evolution.

Are all of us on Mother Earth intended to get to that state?

Yes, it's the cycle of existence. For some, it takes longer. For others, less. It's relative because for us time doesn't exist. Only eternity and limitless expressions or potentials.

I guess I cannot be the same person after receiving higher knowledge.

No, dear, you are moving forward toward your greatness.

Deep thanks, Masters, for assisting me.

That is how it works. We coexist and want the evolution of all.

Anything else for now, Masters? Any other message?

Continue giving what makes you happy to share; that is true giving and existing. You are giving life, light, love, and hope to all. You ignite their hearts with love, joy, peace, and good will.

NINETY

THE MIRROR

Divine Masters, hello! I am here before you to embrace you. I feel honored for our journey together. What do you want to reveal tonight for the good of all?

THE MASTERS SPEAK:

That everything is moving in an orderly fashion—shifting at high frequency.

What do you mean, Masters, what is moving?

The whole.

How does this relate to our lives?

Because of relativity.

Remember, there is entanglement within the matrix. When there is order within you, there is order around you. You are a mirror projecting your reality.

So, ask, what is the reality you want to live? Organize and balance your inner self first and you will experience order and balance outside you. Seamlessly connect both realities.

NINETY-ONE

THE AKASHIC RECORDS

What are the Akashic Records?

THE MASTERS SPEAK:

They are the knowledge of all expressions of creation—its principles, laws, forces, complexities, and memory of each potential in the infinite matrix of existence. In the Akashic Records, all is sustained and clearly understood; there is no veil of confusion, no illusion, nor separation. The ones who access the Akashic Records understand the truth of existence, the purpose and process of evolution.

How do we access these Akashic Records, Masters? Who has access to these records?

The ones in expansion, in search of their truth, origin, and essence have access to them. We told you, those in expansion always attain more truth and higher knowledge to use and apply in their journeys into greatness. The deeper within that you travel and the more attuned you are with your inner truth, the clearer your path into the Akashic Records will be.

These codes of information are imprinted within the subatomic layer of your intracellular expression. All is contained within you.

So, why search for the information in higher realms? I'm guessing the Akashic Records are in higher realms. Is that true?

No, dear, the Akashic Records are in the boundless space of eternity. Your true self is also boundless and eternal. So, you don't have to go anywhere but to your inner true self to discover, see, and understand the codes, principles, and truths that rule everything in existence.

Masters, the Akashic Records, are our own truth of existence accessible to us by knowing and acknowledging our true essence, the soul, right?

Yes, contained in the most intrinsic expression of the self.

To access the Akashic Records, do we need to have a brilliantly pure mind and an open, attuned heart to take the journey of self-recognition and self-knowledge?

Yes. You start the journey within by detaching yourself from the limitations of your mind, your fears, and your illusions. Free yourself of the chains of limited existence. Open to the truth of your nonphysical self, which exists in the eternal now of creation.

Masters, is there any specific practice that we can do to access the Akashic Records?

Surrender to the eternal void of creation and set an intention for this higher knowledge to be revealed to you. Set the intention to recognize the codes and information of existence.

NINETY-TWO

ATTUNEMENT

Good morning, Divine Masters of Truth. What do you want to show me today?

THE MASTERS SPEAK:

Attunement.

Attunement is the congruency between your rhythm and the rhythm of all in creation. Attune yourself first with your rhythm: the rhythm of your breath, of your heart, and of all the other micro-universes that exist within you. After you have attuned yourself within yourself, you will be in sync with the rhythm of nature and life.

As a result of this, other beings attuned within themselves will be aligned with you. Attunement works like a magnet. There is a recognition of like energies. Order recognizes order. Order is the way you can start to grow a community of conscious beings around you.

When you are attuned, nothing distorts your inner order, your balance. There is only acceptance of the experience in each now. Existence becomes easy and simple, an effortless flow, a movement towards greatness and oneness.

What else is there to know about attunement?

Attunement is related to the sound of your inner being. It's being in balance with your rhythm of expression, the uniqueness of your reality as it is occurring in the now. Each beat of your heart expresses a new reality in time. Each breath you breathe is also an expression of a reality in time. These events are unique expressions of your potential.

Knowing and respecting the particularity of your intrinsic self and embracing the unique events occurring within you will give you a better understanding of your truth.

Masters, what daily practices should we to do for attunement?

Close your eyes.
Breathe in, breathe out.
Breathe in light, breathe out peace.
Stay in your inner silence.

Place your attention in your heart. Feel its rhythm and, at the same time, follow the rhythm of your breath.

Embrace the sensation of peace, order, and balance and start feeling, sensing, and visualizing how your cells, tissues, and entire system operate in sync.

Stay there and sense how your whole system is bathed in peace, balance, and order. Following your own rhythm, recognize the feeling of all the functions of your system being one at the same pace. In unison. This will give you the experience of your intrinsic expression. The convergence of rhythms within you is the attunement of yourself.

Thank you for offering us this tool to evolve our consciousness.

NINETY-THREE

THE HIGHER REALMS

THE MASTERS SPEAK:

The higher realms are frequencies of energy organized for a collective knowledge and purpose. There is no separation, no status, no gender in them. We collide in beingness and exist by the law of oneness.

Forgive my ignorance. Are the higher realms the same as dimensions, Masters?

Yes, dear!

And is God the highest realm of all?

God is oneness. It is the supreme forces aligned at will. God is all expressions of potentials and realities expressed at once.

Will all of those living in the third dimension experience the higher realms?

Yes, dear, you already have done so, and you will continue to. It is part of the cycle of existence. It is your right of existence to experience all of them and receive support from us for your evolution. We coexist.

NINETY-FOUR

PURPOSEFUL LIVING AND GIVING

THE MASTERS SPEAK:

It is enough for you to be and to "give away." Align with your essence, discover your gifts, and share them with grace and with generosity for the purpose of common fulfillment. Expand yourself by elevating your frequency. Start from the heart and spread it outwardly.

Recognize yourself as a spark of the divine light and radiate this essence to the entire universe. Integrate and live that truth of your own nature, then your life will evolve with meaning.

Live from the heart, acknowledging your limitless potential and sharing the expression of all your potentials with joy and a deep desire to grow, expand, and nurture the collective.

Ask yourself, every day:

- Who am I today?"
- "What gives joy and fulfillment to my heart and easiness to my living?"
- "How can I evolve or what are the evolutive choices for me?"
- "How can I impact others in their evolutionary process today?"
- "What gift can I share effortlessly and feel happy within by doing so?"
- "Which simple expression of myself can be a gift to others?" (Perhaps it is being present and/or listening with awareness, a small gesture of kindness, or words of wisdom.)

Be present and aware of your own reality in order to be able to engage in the realities of others and serve as a factor of expansion for them.

Masters, are you saying that these are daily self-inquiries to live purposefully with fulfillment?

Yes, dear. Living on purpose is about recognizing your essence first. Everything starts within.

NINETY-FIVE

CALMNESS

Beloved Masters of Love and Happiness, I am ready and eager to receive your wisdom. What is important for me and the world to receive from you today?

THE MASTERS SPEAK:

Calmness. Achieve this state by placing your awareness on your breath, feeling the ordered, rhythmic sound of your breathing, and embracing your inner silence as the voice of the Divine. Enjoy that silence as the music of your heart. Nourish yourself through the process of inner balance that imprints peace and order within you.

Calmness is a state of emergence. It is a passive-active state in which your nervous system reenergizes and balances itself. The more often you dive into calmness, the more wisely responsive you'll be.

How do we cultivate calmness on a daily basis?

Close your eyes and center yourself.
Breathe in, breathe out.
Breathe in the light of Source, breathe out love.
Breathe in love, breathe out harmony.
Breathe in love, breathe out peace.
Breathe in love, breathe out calmness.

Stay there. Listen to the rhythmic sound of your breath and feel its sensations. Let a feeling of peace and stillness pervade you.

Bathe in your inner stillness, silence, and peace.

Rejoice in the calmness of being present with your true self.

When ready, open your eyes and take that state of inner ease, inner confidence, and calmness to your movement into your life. Remember to dive into this practice often. Its power is cumulative. In time, it will give you ease, sharpness, and equanimity to respond.

NINETY-SIX

THE CONNECTION OF ALL

Beloved Divine Masters of Light assisting me and others on this planet, thanks for your support. What do you wish to reveal to us today?

THE MASTERS SPEAK:

The connection of all.
Listen to the waves crashing. What do they tell you?

To be patient and to trust that everything is in order. They tell me to love and nourish, to stay aligned with the truth of my heart and focus on my goals, to love myself unconditionally and search the truth of my existence, to be committed to work towards my truth and happiness, evolution and greatness.

Hey, hey! Stay awake and be heart-centered.

Thanks, Divine Masters, for reminding me to stay aligned with my truth and evolution.

Breathe, breathe, it will give you easiness.
Be silence, be peace.
Be love, be nourishment.
Leave your ego aside and relate to everyone from the heart.

What should I do with all the love I feel within?

Bathe in it and let others bathe in it too. Life is for sharing who you really are: love and truth.

How can I serve the good of all today?

Smile, love, give. Be wise, be humble, and only see the potential and good in everyone. This approach leads to expansion. Truth is shared and love and greatness are lived.
Be peaceful.
When you are in silence and centered in your heart, ask yourself: What is my inner voice telling me? What do I truly desire to be? How do I want to exist? How do I want to give? And your path will be clear, easy, purposeful, joyful, fulfilling, and victorious.
Say, "Divine Love, may I give myself in devotion to love and greatness. May I be a presence of love, joy, peace,

wisdom, and spiritual expansion to all with whom I relate with today."

NINETY-SEVEN

SYMBOLISM

THE MASTERS SPEAK:

Symbolism is a shared language that enables the collective to communicate and relate. Despite these benefits, these are not the true purpose of symbols.

A symbol is the expression of a potential or reality. It is meant to be a reflection or representation of that potential, so it can transmit the real information of what the real object or reality is—of its inherent qualities. For a symbol to be effective, and touch hearts and minds, there has to be congruence between the essence of the potential (or reality) and the symbol that expresses the truth of that potential.

Masters, why are we talking about symbolism?

In order that you may use it to create a healthy society and achieve greatness, evolution, and happiness.

I see. As a conscious society, how may we use symbolism for the good of all?

There has to be truthfulness in the use of symbols. They must not be used for the purpose of misconception, separation, degradation of the essence of the self, or to produce conflict. Symbols are meant to be tools of knowingness, of expansion of the human race, of sharing talents, of engaged societies, and of evolution.

Not weapons.

Can we use this concept of the congruency of symbols to improve our daily lives?

Yes, by staying truthful about your perception of the essence of the symbol. Acknowledge what a symbol represents to you from the purity of your heart and the brilliance of your mind without allowing the fog of a cloudy mind or an exalted ego to disguise the true essence of the symbol. If you are not truthful with yourself about your perception, then a symbol can be misunderstood.

Mischief can be made through egotistical and depleting uses of symbols. Symbols can promote harmony, evolution, reality, and fairness.

NINETY-EIGHT

AMNESTY

My dear Divine Masters, I'm honored and grateful to receive your light and wisdom. I want to give love unconditionally. I want to embrace all the complements as one, as the limitless expression of one truth, the truth of existence. The truth of the self.

What specific topic do you want to reveal today?

THE MASTERS SPEAK:

Amnesty. This is the ability to see the good in others and forgive the acts of others beyond the limiting ego, the ability to be compassionate with the truth and reality of others.

Amnesty liberates the suffering of the "measured" and judged ones, of the ones processed by the rules and precepts of the limited mind and altered ego.

Why are you showing me amnesty, Masters?

To open your heart so you may understand and accept all realities. Leave aside the mind and ego when trying to understand the realities of others. You are all engaged in evolution of the self into truth. The truth of existence.

How could you judge your own nature effectively? How could you judge others for mastering themselves and taking the paths they take to find their greatest selves?

It takes many changes—continuous rebirth—to master yourselves. Do your best to see others through the eyes of your heart.

NINETY-NINE

RESOLUTION OF THE SELF

Masters, what message do you have for the world today?

THE MASTERS SPEAK:

Breathe, hold, liberate.

Stay in the now.

Be still and enjoy the silence around you and the peace within you.

The peace of silence and the wisdom of life resides in that stillness. Enjoy the silence within, as it is nourishment for the system, music for the heart, love for the self.

The true self has a deep desire to emerge and succeed in expressing the qualities of the heart and the brilliance of the mind. Empowered by the strength that comes from within, from the deep memory of the body, and the desire of the self to fulfill its evolutionary aims, you can achieve true satisfaction and contentment.

How do we keep our level of resolution up?

By being in the now, acknowledging the power of the heart, and allowing the brilliance of the mind to guide your actions. Set an intention to stay grounded in the strength of your essence and in the perfection of the systems of the body. Trust the body's inner force, which seeks order, syntropy, and evolution.

Is there a daily practice or set of practices to do to maintain our resolution?

Yes, dear! Ground yourself by touching the soil.

While you are grounding, close your eyes and breathe in the force of life, breathe out easiness.

Inhale the light of the Source, exhale harmony.

Inhale life force and take it to your solar plexus, visualizing and sensing your solar plexus as functioning like a power plant. Visualize that its capacity to generate, propel, and give is limitless. Sense that the energy coming out of your solar plexus ignites the life of your physical system , Mother Earth and radiates to the cosmos and beyond. Visualize this energy as a powerful flame that radiates out from your solar plexus into eternity.

In this way, you are acknowledging, imprinting, memorizing, and strengthening your personal capacity to emerge, to create, to move forward, and to give shape and life to your deepest desires.

Here is some "homework."

Pause, let go.

Put a hand over your heart.

Breathe in and breathe out from your heart.

Stay there, be there.

Rejoice in being there.

ONE HUNDRED

AWAKENING TO LOVE

THE MASTERS SPEAK:

In awakening to love:
Be love.
Be you.
Be joy.
Be smiles.
Be wisdom.
Be inclusive.
Be all.
See all.
Savor all as one.
Play as one.
Indulge in the gifts of the heart and the wisdom of the soul.

I will, Masters, thank you.

ONE HUNDRED-ONE

THE JOY OF EXISTENCE

THE MASTERS SPEAK:

The joy of existence is always felt in the heart and expressed through the voice of the heart and the laughter of the self. Joy's truthfulness is contagious and impactful. The purity of joy's frequency pervades all, propels all, and inspires everyone.

The joy of existence is to love yourself above all and to understand your right to live, to evolve, and to celebrate the fulfillment of your deep desires and the accomplishments of your heart. It is to rejoice in the virtue of love because you understand that love is your inner potential. It is to bathe yourself in the ocean of creation and soak in the magnificence of life, take from it, live in it, and share it openly from your heart.

The joy of life is to be worthy of all because you are already all. You are one.

Feel the joy of life in every breath, in every blink, in every swallow, in every now, in every encounter, in every experience of the self, in every creation of your heart, in every manifestation of your inner strength.

Be joyful, be vital, be great.

Be laughter of the heart.

Be music of the heart.

Be love of the heart.

Be the joy of the heart.

Be the flame of the heart.

ONE HUNDRED-TWO

BLESSINGS

My Divine Masters, I am ready to receive from you. What do you have to share?

THE MASTERS SPEAK:

Magnificence. A profuse fountain of blessings available for you to bathe in and partake from. Use this fountain of blessings to nourish the depth of your being and to vibrate with joy in your hearts and shine your light throughout the world.

How do we share our magnificence?

Simply by opening your heart and exposing your pure self and the boundless treasure chest that is your heart. Share the blueprint of who you are.

Magnificence is all around. Turn around, look, and you will see it. Dive into the ocean and savor it. Breathe and sense it. Sit in silence and hear it. Go for a walk in a garden or forest and smell it. Immerse yourself in the vastness of creation, the grandeur of the sky, and your inner being. You are complex and simple. Look at the tiny cells of your bodies and at your brain and organ systems. These are magnificent. From the core of Mother Earth to infinite consciousness itself magnificence is everywhere.

Are magnificence and abundance the same?

No, magnificence is the way creation expresses its potential. It's expressed and given to you in the form of gifts so beautifully wrapped that they will leave you awestruck.

Abundance is how limitless creation expresses its potential for you to partake in, live from, manifest, and share. Abundance is how magnificently creation is offered to you to live in and live for.

Then, could we say that magnificence is quality and abundance is quantity?

Yes. The human mind defines and measures. Both can also be seen as an expression of reality.

ONE HUNDRED-THREE

LIFE AND ETERNITY

THE MASTERS SPEAK:

Life is a continuous movement of energy, of forces coexisting in permanent feedback, until one day they manifest in a harmonious, orderly manner that is aligned with nature.

What is the difference between life and eternal existence?

The unfolding reality of the mind is life. This is the condensation of the expression of energy to materialize the forces of energy itself. Life is measurable, life is palpable, life is touchable, life is sensed, life is seen in the confines of the mind.

Eternal existence is unmeasurable since it is boundless. It's a limitless expression or potential which is energy itself.

It's all and it's nothing after being all. Eternal existence is all the potentials of energy expressing in the eternal now and composed by each now.

This is kind of difficult for my human mind to process, Masters! It seems complex to me.

Life or existence is hard to process when it is experienced from the limited point of view of the ego self. The ego doesn't allow us to see all the potential and possibilities of creation that are available to the boundless true self.

When the ego is involved, there are restrictions imposed on the human mind.

Masters, is there a practical aspect to these two concepts?

There is only one reality that is the source of them. That source is all, with the memory of all that exists. Be the secret, live by the secret, and work as needed.

Do you want love? Be love.

Do you want joy? Be joy.

Do you want wisdom? Be wise.

Do you want purpose? Be purposeful.

Be life, be you.

ONE HUNDRED-FOUR

THE GREATNESS OF CREATION

I embrace your presence and higher knowledge with deep gratitude, Divine Beings of Light. What do you want to show me and the world today?

THE MASTERS SPEAK:

The greatness of creation. Its chants have a soothing effect. We rejoice in its delicate frequencies. Wake up to life, wake up to love, and more.

Take a moment for self-alignment, recognition, and attunement with the rhythm of creation. Take a moment for reshaping and reordering your reality. Continue vibrating with the qualities of the heart and listening to the voice of your soul.

There are changes taking place. A collective rebirth is occurring and creating nations of greatness.

And what is my duty in this moment? How may I serve you and humankind?

Travel within, experience your true self. Be and give from your heart. Be the method of simplicity and share the method of simplicity. Trust. Keep organizing and you will be ready for our mission together. Stay located in your heart.

Thank you, Masters, for assisting me in honoring my higher purpose.

Smile, smile. Yes, smile. It's a magnet for blessings.

Infinite thanks, Divine Beloved Masters.

<3<3<3

THE SIMPLICITY OF ALL THINGS

What do you want to show or teach me today, Masters?

THE MASTERS SPEAK:

The simplicity of all things.

It is simple to sit in silence and pay attention to your heart.

It is simple to let the wind caress your skin with its wisdom.

It is simple to enjoy bird songs.

Breathe in, breathe out.

Breathe in, breathe out.

Enjoy the presence of the Divine within you.

CONTEMPLATION

THE MASTERS SPEAK:

Contemplation is a practice for inner awareness and recognition of all that exists. It's the enjoyment of creation from a nonjudgmental state, using your subtle awareness to recognize the truth that reigns outside and inside your body.

Contemplation is a profound practice of bringing your self-awareness into alignment with all that exists. It's a subtle communication or communion with all that exists. Contemplation makes space for all the potentials of creation to express themselves and for you to embrace them with total awareness, openness, and gratitude. It is an opportunity for an encounter of unconditional love, as there is no expectation and no controlling. It's simply a mutual surrender. Whenever there is surrendering, all possibilities unfold. Beings awaken. Life shines brightly and magnificently.

Through contemplation, you are releasing yourself into the hands of God and allowing yourself to be held by the forces of creation. It is peaceful, it's truthful, it's soothing.

Contemplation is seeing your own truth in the mirror of life. And recognizing that the truth you see outside you is the same as the reality you embody. Because of this mirroring effect, contemplation is a practice that can restore your inner balance and harmony. It is a demonstration of self-love. Through contemplation we are able to understand our own rhythm, our own cycles.

What more is there to know about contemplation, Masters?

Be still and peace will reign.

How do we practice contemplation, Masters?

Sit still with your eyes open and direct your gaze forward between your eyes. Always in front. This will help you stay in the now and the reality that is being experienced or contemplated.

Have an easy gaze and easy breathing. Allow your breath to be slower and shallower than normal.

Relax into the now with stillness and calmness and be open to the reality you are gazing at, embracing its truth without judgment.

Stay there and enjoy the peace within, the communion with all. Allow a soothing feeling to permeate your whole being. Be peace, be silence. Be love, be soul.

The practice is not about what you are contemplating but becoming one with it. A feeling of connectedness and peace and an experience of oneness will unfold.

Divine Masters of Light, thank you for your presence.

It is only love pouring over you from us.

What a gift! What a blessing it is!

ONE HUNDRED-SEVEN

BEING PEACE

Divine Beings of Light from the Higher Realms who are assisting us in our evolution, thanks. What is in your consciousness today that you want to share for the good of all?

THE MASTERS SPEAK:

Breathe, stay in stillness. Stay calm. Rejoice in the stillness and peace within. Receive the blessings of life. You are worthy of them.

I am. Yes, I am.

Say: "In silence I am with all. I experience the Divine."
Inhale love, exhale peace. Peace is who you really are.
Inhale love, exhale harmony. Harmony is who you really are.

Inhale divine light, exhale light. Light is who you really are.

Inhale divine light, exhale oneness. Oneness is who you really are.

Be oneness, live oneness.

Rejoice in the depths of the self, in the peace that resides within, in the light of the soul, in the beats of your heart. Be peace and spread peace.

ONE HUNDRED-EIGHT

REJOICE

I feel so happy and grateful, Divine Masters. There is so much love in my heart.

THE MASTERS SPEAK:

This is the truth of your existence. Love.

This truth is only real within. In the silence of the self, in the treasures of the heart.

So, are you inviting me to sit in silence, Masters?

Yes, dear. Be peace, be you, be and enjoy the voice of the soul. Rejoice in the purity of the soul and in the beauty and generosity of your heart.

I will, dear Masters. Honestly, I'm trying to do that every day because it gives me joy and peace and keeps me centered in my own truth.

That is where you want to be. In your truth—and to realize it. It is a privilege to see and know the Divine in yourself.

AFTERWORD

My journey with higher consciousness has continued to unfold since these messages were channeled through me. I feel a deep desire for love and to lead a conscious life; and I feel called to be aware of my relationship with myself and how I treat my body. I believe many people share these desires and callings.

Here is my takeaway from communicating with the Masters of the Truth of Love and Happiness on a near daily basis for over a year. You have a choice whether to define yourself in terms of outer expectations or inner needs. The journey of self-mastery and awakening is about traveling first into the depths of the ocean of life that you are and then bringing what you find there out into the world. Acknowledging yourself gives you the ability to recognize and partake in everything that life is offering you.

I'd like to leave you with my understanding and integration of the importance of living connected to your heart, which is this: No matter what, even in moments when your outer reality shakes you, breathe, center your awareness in your heart, and reconnect with the aliveness and beauty of your true self. In every moment, regardless of the toughness or ease of your life, choose to love yourself, abide in happiness, and take the opportunity to be in charge of your reality—in charge of your emotions. Decide to be the generator of the truth you want to live and share.

You may say: "Yes, this seems easy, but when life is against me and rocks my world, how can I stay calm and in charge?"

That's the moment when you're being called to get in contact with your body. You're being invited to feel it and to recognize how all is sustained in perfect order and harmony within it. If you accept the invitation and follow the calling, you will realize the full extent of your power. Control of your life cannot really be given away.

What do you want? What do you want to give? How do you want to live? Fulfillment of desire starts with knowing what you're seeking. Own your desire. Make it yours. Feel it in the deepest places of yourself, in your body. Feel the emotions that represent your wanting.

Also visualize that which you desire. Create a movie in your mind about its attainment and watch it over and over again, treating it as if it were a reality to you. Soak in the essence of what you deeply desire. Allow yourself to experience sincere, profound gratitude for it. The magic of manifestation, of creating realities, will handle the rest.

It's rewarding to know that nothing is off limits—to feel your limitless power, worth, and connection to all. This inspires in most people an immense feeling of gratitude and awe.

My personal connection to higher consciousness has come from my devotion to living in my heart and experiencing its qualities, like self-love, joy, and gratitude, every day. It also comes from having the intention to be a presence of love, wellbeing, and spiritual expansion for others. I have done my best to adhere to the guidance that the Masters of Truth gave me to share with you and the results for me personally have been remarkable.

My commitment now is to see the good in everything and everyone, and to be of assistance to those who are interested in mastering themselves, integrating higher frequency energy, and evolving, based on their own needs for self-realization.

At the end of the day, of all the principles described in this book, the two that I believe are the ultimate keys for a life of connection, of simplicity, of fulfillment, of happiness, and of freedom are forgiveness and self-love. If you do nothing else, work on those principles.

To the best of your ability, love yourself and do for yourself that which you'd like divine consciousness to do for you. Travel within and acknowledge the wisdom of your higher self. Let it guide you. Feel and express yourself from your heart. Discover and offer yourself the most fulfilling dream, goal, or divine purpose you have in your heart.

Also, do your best to forgive yourself and others. Let the qualities of the heart pervade your thinking and your behavior in every interaction.

Spread your spirit, your joy, your knowledge with humility, wisdom, magnificence, and grace. Give with the goal of elevating your essence and bringing happiness to others.

ACKNOWLEDGMENTS

Foremost, I thank the Masters of the Truth of Love and Happiness for collaborating with me. Without you, there would be no book. It is a privilege and honor to help spread your messages. I would also like to thank my higher self for creating such a beautiful opportunity for me—it has been transformative.

I acknowledge and offer special thanks to my beloved daughter, Nicole, who played a key role in the development of this project. She unconditionally embraced the knowledge I downloaded and helped me transcribe it with genuine commitment. Ours was a shared journey of self-expansion.

Thanks to my son, Milton, for his admiration and support and for always adding a spark of joy to my life.

I also acknowledge and immensely appreciate my husband, Milton, for welcoming and taking up this knowledge as an elixir of wisdom for his own life and personal evolution. I am grateful for his generous and continuous support of me as I focus on the achievement of my goals.

Thank you to my father, as well, who has inspired me to express my truth and knowledge. As a passionate storyteller and avid student of history who seduces his audiences with his liveliness and character, he's an excellent role model.

In addition, I feel deep gratitude to the friends who listened when I would read messages in our gatherings; they received the insights with so much interest, appreciation, gratitude, and devotion that I knew I was on the right track and had captured invaluable messages.

I am indebted to Kenna and others who patiently helped me with my technological issues during the transcription of the material.

I'd like to recognize and thank my energy healer, Cathy Fernandez, who has been a masterful guide for me and a translator of some of the downloads I've channeled. She has given me tools to manage my energy so that it is possible to be available for this work.

I also feel admiration and profound gratitude for various masters who have crossed my path during my lifelong journey of self-realization. Their wisdom, techniques, and concepts, which I have experienced through their books, retreats, and certification courses, have helped me evolve into the woman I am today.

I give special recognition to my editor and publishing consultant, Stephanie Gunning, founder of Gunning Writer Works, who has produced numerous bestselling and award-winning books, for putting her expertise, creativity, sense of humor, and keen knowledge into the editing and completion of this book and helping me in the fulfillment of my life purpose.

Thanks to my publicists, Bobby Coimbra and David Borges, and Creative Director Héctor Chacón Hänsen from Soho Square Coimbra-Ogilvy Group, for coming into this project at the right moment with creativity and strategies that will help me spread the message I so deeply wish to share with the world. I am very grateful to Héctor for designing the front cover of the book and drawing the key illustration that is featured on the cover and the interior.

Many thanks also to Adriana de Hassan, my Spanish translator, and Ana del Corral Londoño, my Spanish editor, who with their ability and beautiful energy polished the manuscript and contributed to the dissemination of this knowledge to the people of my beloved Venezuela and other Spanish-speaking cultures.

RESOURCES

Thank you for reading this book. It is an honor to be of service to you by sharing the wisdom of the Masters of the Truth of Love and Happiness with you, and I hope you will help me spread their insights on the method of simplicity and the thirteen laws of existence further. To assist you in cultivating a magical lifestyle based upon this guidance, I have created some additional resources. Please use these in good health and with abiding joy.

1–CONNECT WITH ME

Website: www.LorenaGodoy.com

Email: books@lorenagodoy.com

Instagram: @lorenasoulconnection

Facebook: @lorenasoulconnection

2–ATTEND AN INDIVIDUAL OR GROUP MEDITATION WORKSHOP WITH ME

Would you like to initiate or expand your practice of meditation? When you study with me, I provide you with a personal mantra (vibration) calculated for you using the methods of the Vedic tradition taught at the Chopra Center for Wellbeing. This mantra will be your vehicle to settle your thoughts and relax your mind so that you can reach deeper states of consciousness.

The meditation course is a space to develop self-knowledge. It is a chance to release physical and emotional stress and improve the quality of our sleep. It also is an opportunity to explore our inner silence, which gives us access to our true essence, our consciousness, and the field of infinite possibilities. Meditations is a trip inward in which we experience a state of infinite peace and joy.

3–COACH WITH ME ONE ON ONE

As your coach, I will hold space for you and accompany you in your journey of personal transformation and awakening to a life of connection to your heart, so you may create and manifest love, abundance, and magic. I will give you tips for intuitive writing and connection to higher consciousness (channeling).

4–INVITE ME TO SPEAK TO YOUR READING OR WRITING GROUP

During our visit, I will share my experience, journey, and knowledge received from higher realms. It's my soul calling and deep desire to spread these messages to elevate ease, self-realization and happiness. A powerful and inspiring way to do this is as a group collectively deepening in the drops of wisdom of *Keys to Love and Happiness*.

5–BUY COPIES IN BULK FOR YOUR ORGANIZATION

Special discounts are available to purchase copies in bulk directly from Lorena Godoy Books. We hope to spread the profound and skillful knowledge of *Keys to Love and Happiness* as widely as possible to create more creative, harmonious, and evolutionary communities.

Email us about your needs at books@lorenagodoy.com

ABOUT THE AUTHOR

LORENA GODOY is a transformational coach and certified meditation teacher who facilitates the internal process of expansion and self-realization of others. She received her training in meditation from the Chopra Center for Wellbeing. Since 2019, she has been channeling messages daily from the Masters of the Truth of Love and Happiness.

Lorena is passionate about the knowledge she has integrated through her mystical experiences. Sharing this wisdom in many forms and venues has become her principal work and life purpose. She feels a profound calling to contribute to the awakening of the collective spiritual consciousness. *Keys to Love and Happiness* is her first book.

Venezuelan in origin, Lorena divides her time between homes in Miami, Florida, and on Margarita Island,

Venezuela, where the peaceful natural setting beside the ocean is appropriate for a life of ease. The energy of the island induces her to travel within in silence, immerse herself in writing, and enjoy a simple life with her loved ones and friends.